DESTINED FOR LIBERTY

DESTINED FOR LIBERTY

The Human Person in the Philosophy of
KAROL WOJTYŁA/JOHN PAUL II

Jarosław Kupczak, O.P.

The Catholic University of America Press
Washington, D.C.

The paper used in this publication meets the minimum require-
ments of American National Standards for Information Science—
Permanence of Paper for Printed Library materials,
ANSI Z39.48–1984.

∞

Library of Congress Cataloging-in-Publication Data

Kupczak, Jaroslaw, 1964–
    Destined for liberty : the human person in the philosophy of
Karol Wojtyla/John Paul II / Jaroslaw Kupczak.
        p.   cm.
    Includes bibliographical references and index.
    1. John Paul II, Pope, 1920—Contributions in philosophy of
agent. 2. Agent (Philosophy)—History—20th century. I. Title.
BD450.K82 2000
199'.438—dc21
99–087156
ISBN 0–8132–0984–6 (cloth : alk. paper)
ISBN 0–8132–0985–4 (pbk. : alk. paper)

Dedicated to my Brethren at the
Dominican House of Studies in Washington, D.C.

CONTENTS

ACKNOWLEDGMENTS

Gratitude and appreciation are due to many in the preparation of this book. First of all I would like to thank Carl A. Anderson, former Dean of the Pontifical John Paul II Institute for Studies on Marriage and Family, for his support and friendship during my studies there.

I am grateful to Professor Kenneth L. Schmitz for his guidance. His example as a gentleman and a Christian philosopher will always be with me. Michael Novak was the first person to encourage me to publish this book. I am also indebted to him for letting me use his essay "Christian Philosophy of Karol Wojtyła" as an introduction. From the beginning, I was supported by the Director of Catholic University of America Press, David J. McGonagle. I am also grateful to Mary and Russell Hittinger for the superb editorial work they have done together. Romanus Cessario, O.P., was always willing to help me with his advice.

I also wish to thank the staff and faculty at the John Paul II Institute, especially Sister Sarah Doser, F.S.E. The reading of the manuscript by Monsignor Robert Sokolowski and Professor Stanisław Grygiel was immensely helpful. Thanks is also due to all who helped me with my English, especially Laura Ingraham, Timothy Bellamah, O.P., Martin Martiny, O.P., and Kevin McGrath, O.P.

Without the generous support of the Knights of Columbus and the Dominican Province of St. Joseph, and most especially the fraternal charity of my brethren at the Dominican House of Studies, this project would never have been possible. To them also goes my gratitude and love.

Jarosław Kupczak, O.P.
Kraków, August 1999

The Christian Philosophy of John Paul II

BY MICHAEL NOVAK

Unless many recent conversations around the country mislead me, intelligent Catholics in significant numbers seem not to be on the same wavelength as Pope John Paul II. In some ways this is odd, because intelligent Catholics usually like an intelligent and articulate pope, and this one is perhaps the most intellectually original, articulate, and prolific pope of the past one hundred years. Some of this discordance results (those who don't cotton to him sometimes suggest) from their very different reading of Vatican II. Some of it results, they say, from very strong feelings of disagreement about particular questions such as women priests, contraception, and celibacy. Many are willing to admit, however, that they simply do not see what this pope is up to—do not follow, and cannot recount, his arguments. To a remarkable extent, in rather wide circles of American Catholicism a certain resistance to John Paul II seems to be the expected attitude. It is sad, I think, to be alive during one of the great pontificates in history and to be in passive opposition to it.

This general lack of insight into why the Pope teaches and acts as he does is apparent in two popular, recent biographies, that by Tad

Szulc and that by Carl Bernstein and Marco Politi, as well as in the recent account *American Catholic* by Charles R. Morris, not to mention
the running commentaries of the late Peter Hebblethewaite.

Nonetheless, it should be possible to set out an account of John
Paul II's method, and to assist readers in grasping the originality of
several of his conceptual achievements, even without attempting to
close the disagreements on particular questions that some Catholics
express. I hope that even those who do not go along with the Pope may
find such an effort of service.

It has often been pointed out, of course, that the Pope was a professional philosopher before he became a bishop, and that he is probably
better identified as belonging to the school of phenomenology than,
say, as a Neo-Thomist. People often said that Paul VI, for example, was
an admirer and even follower of Jacques Maritain, but while there are
points of contact with Maritain in Wojtyła's work, one could not read-
ily understand him within Maritain's framework.

One key to understanding Karol Wojtyła, I think, is that he is first
of all a poet and dramatist. His sensibility is that of an artist. He is
sensitive, feels things deeply, responds instantly to persons and situations through his emotions, takes things in as wholes, and learns
quickly from concrete experience. He trusts experience more than
words. He likes to reflect on concrete wholes, as an artist would, in
order to allow their inner form to emerge subtly and slowly. He is not
in a rush to slash, channel, contort, or ignore parts of these concrete
wholes in concepts or systems. These dispositions led him at a very
young age to find both release and congenial techniques in phenomenological method, particularly as he found it in Max Scheler (d.
1928), the philosopher par excellence of the feelings.

It is a rare American, of course, who is helped by hearing the term
phenomenology. I have seen even professional philosophers blanch on

being asked to offer a thumbnail sketch of phenomenology, and listened as well-travelled journalists approached even the pronunciation of the term the way they would approach a three-foot-wide ditch: back up a few steps, take a deep breath, and lunge.

Simply put, phenomenology is a sustained effort to bring back into philosophy everyday things, concrete wholes, the basic experiences of life as they come to us. It wishes to recapture these quotidian realities from the empiricists, on the one hand, who analyze them into sense data, impressions, chemical compositions, neural reactions, etc., and from the idealists, on the other hand, who break them up into ideal types, categories, and forms. When girl meets boy (as Rebecca in Genesis first sees Isaac coming toward her across the field), the psychologist may be interested in her prior relation to her father, and Kant may be concerned that her attachment to the categorical imperative may be going wobbly in the face of teleological hedonism. But the phenomenologist is interested in her experience of love as a concrete whole, in the many strands that there move her. How much is involved? How many elements make up the whole? How does this whole of experience differ from others she has known? What does her own heart tell her is lacking—or fulfilling—within it? This example suggests why, despite its cumbersome name, phenomenological method has had some of its greatest successes in the arts and aesthetics, as in the work of Wojtyła's friend from Kraków, the philosopher Roman Ingarden. A certain dramatic texture is inherent within it, and it has a taste of "the real."

As an actor who had played men moved by both great and tender passions on the stage, and as a dramatist and poet who had tried to create scenes in which powerful emotions and rich experiences could be relived by others, Wojtyła found Max Scheler to be in part a wonderful guide to the panoply of meanings and values embodied in the rich world of human feelings. Perhaps a contemporary parallel on the American scene today might be the recent book by James Q. Wilson, *The Moral Sense*. In the end, though, Wojtyła found Scheler not a complete guide to human experience and feeling; in his own life, there were elements Scheler did not know of or explain.

I am not able to read the Polish texts of Wojtyła's Lublin lectures, in which as a young professor he recounted both his appreciation of and disappointments in Scheler's work. But I have been enormously helped by a brilliant doctoral thesis produced at John Paul II Institute for Studies on Marriage and Family last year by a young Dominican from Kraków, Jarosław Kupczak. According to Kupczak, Scheler was allergic to feelings of obligation, and determined to show that Kant was wrong in grounding morals in duty, rather than in feelings. Wojtyła knew from his own experience that feelings are very important to the moral life and wonderfully subtle teachers; they often lead us to insights that the intellect itself is at first blind to or resistant to. On the other hand, he had himself experienced moments when he felt the heavy hand of duty upon reluctant feelings, and knew he had to act even when he was afraid and experiencing dread.

More to the point, perhaps, feelings are something that "happen" to us; in a way, we are receivers of feelings, we suffer them, they come unbidden. But Wojtyła had also known moments when he knew he had to take charge of his own life, to will something, to make something new happen, to become the agent of his own decisions. Here, too, he found Scheler too passive.

Before studying Scheler, Wojtyła had also—during World War II and just afterwards—been introduced to the writings of Thomas Aquinas, through a textbook produced by a transcendental Thomist who had studied at Louvain with Désiré Cardinal Mercier and Joseph Maréchal. For two long months Wojtyła struggled with the density and abstraction and complexity of the thing—what a way to meet both Aquinas/Aristotle and Kant at the same time, under Nazi occupation and after some years of hard manual labor and work in the clandestine theater! When Wojtyła had climbed high enough through the thickets to see where he was, and get a sense of the terrain, he had two very strong feelings: first, he had found a way of articulating some of his most important experiences (of inner searching and conversion, of will, of agency, of call and obligation, of growth and becoming, e.g.) and, second, he saw that Thomism was stronger on nature than on human nature—it lacked a full theory of consciousness, interiority, and even the feelings. It had strengths the moderns lack, but it was weak in some places where modernity demands strength. He thought it might be his task to contribute to bringing to the Thomistic patrimony a sense of interiority, a theory that included consciousness in its full range: somatic, vegetative, neural, emotional, passional, imaginative, intellectual, in the will.

At Lublin in the mid-1950s, then the freest and most independent university in the entire East, behind the Iron Curtain, Wojtyła lectured on Hume, Kant, Scheler, and other figures in the history of ethical thought, while slowly developing his own thesis on human agency and creativity, which was eventually published (more as notes-in-progress than as the rounded book he would have wished to produce—he was working on it even during sessions of the Vatican Council) under the title *The Acting Person*. If we now imagine Wojtyła working at his desk in St. Peter's as a young bishop during the years 1961–65, this might be a good moment to pause to introduce one other major strand in his way of thinking.

During his earlier stay in Rome for doctoral studies at the Angelicum from 1946–48, where he wrote a thesis on St. John of the Cross and St. Thomas Aquinas on faith, Karol Wojtyła was much taken with the argument on Christian philosophy launched by Etienne Gilson. According to Gilson, while maintaining its own methodological autonomy, philosophy had been and could continue to be enriched by questions posed for it by Christian faith. For example, the concept of "person" had first been developed in the context of the doctrine on the Trinity, and the concept of will arose from questions posed in the New Testament about doing what we will not, and not doing what we will. The notion of "conscience" and many other notions also arose because of difficulties that arose from reflections on Christian experience in the light of inadequate secular theories.

For Wojtyła, the most impressive problem posed for him by Christian experience in our time—a problem arising directly from biblical texts and from his experience of our time—is the question of freedom. For him, the question is first of all interior, but under the Nazis and the Communists he could not help noticing that freedom also has a political, even an economic, dimension, and a cultural as well as a personal dimension. It is not easy to explain how some men seem to yield up their freedom to threats or even to the mass sentiment surrounding them, while others like Maximilian Kolbe are able to remain fearless masters of their own decisions. Wojtyła has always been fascinated by the agency open to humans, the ability to—and the call to—take charge of one's own life. Ironically, of course, this "taking charge" often means remaining receptive to calls of grace, keeping oneself out of comfortable ruts so as to be disposed to going wherever God calls, even if one feels one has not the strength.

The point is, unlike kittens or dogs, human lives are not bound by iron circles of instinct and routine; our minds and wills are always open to fresh and immediate inspirations of grace, new calls to conversion and action, even if only in the manner and intensity with which we attend to everyday duties. In each staccato second the human spirit is open, free, creative, receptive, and ready to act in fresh ways.

Twice in his life, Wojtyła requested permission to enter the Carmelites, the order that nourished St. John of the Cross, St. Teresa of Avila, and St. Therese of Lisieux, three of the greatest doctors of the interior life, especially the life of inner darkness of spirit and naked, abandoned faith. All three, too, each in a different way, stressed the utility of humble daily routines and humdrum quotidian activities for poverty of spirit and acts of love for God and others. To fail to see the extent to which Wojtyła's soul is Carmelite is to miss a great deal, indeed. This means that he sees grace in all the things of nature, and all the things of nature as whisperers of grace. He tries always to be in the presence of God, even when (perhaps especially when) sharing a good joke. Like most Poles, he likes being made to laugh; and his friend Father Józef Tischner, for example, has a reputation of being one of the best joke-tellers in a nation of joke-tellers. Laughter, even more than sorrow, is part of the splendor of being; Poland knows more than its share of both.

At the Second Vatican Council, Wojtyła worked closely with Henri de Lubac, and he and the famous Jesuit became good friends, as the latter testifies in his memoirs. Wojtyła also shares with de Lubac the conviction that the concept of pure nature—apart from the fall and grace—is a mere hypothetical, which does not and never did exist. Today everything that is is graced, wounded though it be by the fall. Both also share a vision of the church as a communion, a "we." It would not be right to say that the views of Wojtyła and de Lubac on these questions are identical, but Wojtyła's views on them are closer to de Lubac's than to those of any other theologian. This helps to explain why the Pope sees so much sacramentality and grace in every land, historical event, and monument—as his talks in every part of the world demonstrate. He reads history and nature sacramentally.

To those brought up thinking about natural law in the way, say, that the great John Courtney Murray did, the Pope's habit of insisting that the human being cannot be understood apart from Jesus Christ may at first seem disconcerting. Yet the Pope is always thinking about the enormous impact of Jesus Christ upon concrete history, including huge geological shifts, so to speak, in the terrain of philosophy itself. To choose Anglo-American examples, even philosophers as disparate as Bertrand Russell and Richard Rorty have candidly admitted that key concepts absolutely central to their own philosophies, such as compassion and solidarity, respectively, derive from the heritage of Jesus Christ, not Greece or Rome or even the Enlightenment. Even such concepts as person, conscience, the dignity of every individual without exception, and individual liberty, Wojtyła notes, arose from sustained reflection on the gospels. In the Pope's thought, the realm of "nature" is thin and hypothetical, indeed, compared to the actual workings of the fall and of grace in real history.

On the other hand, Wojtyła has never hesitated to speak a secular language to those who are secular. As a philosopher, he is quite accustomed to discussing problems without appeal to the language or premises of faith. In the old days during his debates with Marxist philosophers, he found it quite possible to turn the Marxist doctrines of labor inside-out through a purely philosophical (phenomenological) examination of the concrete experience of the steelworker in Nowa Huta and the fisherman in Gdańsk. He is not one of those Christians who cannot think unless he quotes biblical texts. When, as on his recent visit to Poland, the Pope speaks privately to the Communist President of the nation, one imagines that he can speak man-to-man in terms the President will have no difficulty understanding, terms that would not have required Christian faith.

In other words, it is not merely that Wojtyła has an unusual facility with many national languages; he also feels at home in and can communicate in a large number of quite different intellectual traditions and disciplinary contexts. One might say that in this way, by a different route, he also observes the protocols of the two different languages of nature and of grace.

The letters of advice that Bishop Wojtyła sent to the Preparatory Commission of the Second Vatican Council may have been the first to suggest the two axial concepts that later were to run through every document of the Council as if lettered in crimson, a kind of conceptual spine: *person* and *community*. These became the axial concepts not only of the document on religious liberty but also of *Lumen Gentium* (on the Church) and *Gaudium et Spes* (on the Church in the Modern World). Wojtyła remembers with special fondness his intimate collaboration on the drafting of the last. Yet Paul VI gave credit to the interventions of Wojtyła on behalf of the document on religious liberty for his last-minute decision that documents must be voted on before the Council closed, when the tactic of the opposition had been to work for irretrievable delay. Paul VI could not turn down the appeal of those suffering behind the Iron Curtain for a strong word about liberty; and the interventions of Wojtyła proved, he told the conservatives, that the issue arose not solely from restless bishops in the secular countries of the West.

As Bishop and as Pope, Wojtyła has been consistent in his belief that Vatican II was an immense grace and marks out God's will for the Church in our time. He rejects projective readings of the Council, however, by which some read into it their own wishes or even fantasies. He asks for a full, balanced, non-selective reading of its documents, rich in their balance and measured reflection. Many in the advanced countries, it seems, have an image of what Vatican II meant that is not based upon actual meditation on the written text. He urges serious inquirers to study the documents in a spirit of prayer and learning. He is not afraid to recommend an attitude of obedience to God, obedience of the sort that led many thousands of priests in his generation to accept martyrdom. The so-called "spirit of Vatican II," I have found myself, is no substitute for getting the doctrine of Vatican II straight from the texts. Re-reading those documents brings surprises on virtually every page.

In the July 1997 issue of *Crisis*, John Crosby points out how much the Pope's teachings on sexual ethics have in common with that of many "progressives"—but also the unnoticed premise that differentiates his teaching from theirs; namely, the phenomenological analysis of action that stresses the unity of body and spirit, and uncovers in consciousness pain at their separation. I do not wish to enter into these controversies here, for my aim is not to argue such matters of substance but, rather, to call attention to the originality of the Pope's way of analyzing matters. Too many, I find, are reacting with resistance to something they do not recognize, without having any guide to help them clarify further the area of dispute. It is not right to allow unnecessary obscurity to persist. Some effort is required, but Wojtyła's reasoning is far more interesting and original than he is being given credit for. Some are judging him entirely within their own categories, a tactic they do not like when others use it against them.

A resident assistant at a supposedly sedate Ivy League university told me how, at freshmen orientation week, representatives of the university threw handfuls of condoms out into the gathered assembly of young men and women fresh from their homes and eager to learn about the university experience, and how they scrambled around on the floor picking up the condoms. Everyone was expected to carry one out, as their ticket to the university experience. Instructions were also passed out for a variety of sexual acts that some of them, at least, did not even care to know about. The rationale for the distribution of condoms was "safety." It was assumed that they would be having sex with people they did not know and could not trust, and probably with multiple partners. In other words, the university expected them to experience a radical separation between their bodily acts and their souls. The weeks to follow were made endurable by the ingestion of large quantities of alcohol and drugs before sex. (Three women in the dorm—a mixed dorm, naturally—were found nude and unconscious in various rooms, including common bathrooms, and in one case outside on the grounds during that term.) Hearing this story, others from other universities have matched it.

Yes, some will say, but within the bonds of matrimony and within a loving permanent relationship, the use of contraceptives is different. No doubt. Yet, Wojtyła points out, the alienation between body and soul remains detectable. However one finally resolves this question in one's own mind, one must say that Wojtyła's analysis hits a worrisome nerve. (It reminds one, too, of the empirical research describing young women who sometimes do not use contraceptives, not because they want to conceive, but because they do not want anything to come between them and the one they actually love; sometimes tragically, they intend this as a sign to him.)

On the question of a celibate clergy, too, it is useful to ask what Wojtyła thinks the priesthood is. When he became a priest and during the forty years afterward, Wojtyła knew that thousands of Polish priests were being killed, sent to labor camps, beaten, and jailed for years at a time, simply for being priests. To be a priest was to be a marked man. In such circumstances, the fact that priests did not have families to support was a blessing. To become a priest was actually, and was regarded as, a brave and manly act. The life to be led was one of poverty, uncertainty, physical discipline, and mortified flesh. A significant part of one's work would be clandestine. One would need to go out at all hours and in all weather. One priest would be clubbed by an anonymous band of thugs, in circumstances that made the act seem not unplanned; another would be approached after mass and struck on the head by a rock swung by a "madman," who would go unpunished. To see the large number of vocations to the priesthood in Poland today, and to witness the manly bearing and high morale of those who enter, is to see the harvesting of countless acts of courage and fidelity.

On matters of social ethics, one well-known U.S. theologian likes to describe Catholic social thought as a triad of "three S's"—Solidarity, Subsidiarity, and Social Justice. To these, John Paul II has added Subjectivity—the human person as subject, as agent, as center of imagination, initiative, and determined will. Against collectivism of all sorts, the Pope counterpoises the self-conscious human subject who pours herself into all that she does. Here, too, he sees the ground for defending rights to private property and to private initiative; and, more basic still, rights to religious and moral liberty. Further, because he sees social justice as rooted in individual subjects, he is also able to defend it as a virtue, a habit of a new and specific sort proper to free men and women, a new seat of social responsibility. In this vein, too, the Pope now places on families—what he calls the domestic church—the new locus of the royal power that the church once vested in kings, the royal obligation of building up the civilization of love. For him, the new *civis* is the married husband and wife, and it is they, not the state, who are the prime bearer of civilizing responsibilities. (Russell Hittinger of the University of Tulsa has tracked this turn in papal thought best.)

Those who wish to pursue further studies in the thought of John Paul II will now be tremendously helped by the magisterial, clear, and profound book of Rocco Buttiglione, *Karol Wojtyla* (Eerdmans Publishing, pp. 384 + xvi), the best study in any language. Buttiglione learned Polish and worked with Wojtyła before the latter became pope. He is much loved and trusted by the pope, who asked Buttiglione to write the brilliant introduction to the third Polish edition *The Acting Person* (1994), which is reprinted in this handsome volume. Many American Catholics, I believe, will be stunned by the intellectual achievement recorded in Buttiglione's study. Like Wojtyła, Buttiglione also shares a great love for America and its tradition of practicality and commonsense, and is able to show connections between phenomenological method and typically American habits of thought.

Since Pope John Paul II has the large vision of a philosopher, he is a little like Leo XIII (1878–1903) in the broad range of the subjects he writes about. It looks now, too, as if his papacy may run as long, or longer. Indeed, if John Paul lives as long as Leo, he will celebrate Easter of the year 2013 in the papacy. Beyond sharing years and range of views, however, I think it can be fairly argued that John Paul II is more professionally trained in a variety of contemporary disciplines than Leo XIII was, more penetrating, more original and—perhaps for that reason—more disturbing.

I know that my friend Hans Kung thinks that Pope John Paul II is very bad for the church, according to Hans' vision of the church. Yet, affection for Hans aside, I think that John Paul II is very good for the church. The church as Hans wants it is not a church I would wish to belong to nor is it, by Hans' own testimony, the church it has always been.

I hope all my progressive friends will forgive me if I close with the ancient Polish prayer, on behalf of Karol Wojtyła: *"May he live a hundred years!"*

Reprinted with permission from *America*, October 1997.

DESTINED FOR LIBERTY

CHAPTER 1

Prologue

I N T H E Y E A R 1 9 9 4 , *Time* magazine chose Pope John Paul II as its "Man of the Year." *Time* explained its choice, noting that the Pope's

popular book and his unpopular diplomacy . . . share one philosophical core: "It always goes back to the sanctity of the human being." . . . In a year when so many people lamented the decline in moral values or made excuses for bad behavior, Pope John Paul II forcefully set forth his vision of the good life and urged the world to follow it. For such rectitude—or recklessness, as his detractors would have it—he is *Time*'s Man of the Year.[1]

John Paul II's vision of the good life is founded on a consistent and profound theory of the human person. The foundations of his Christian anthropology were in place before Karol Wojtyła became Bishop of Rome. Completed after his election to the papal office, his theory forms "a complete Christian alternative to the humanistic philosophies of the twentieth century—Marxism, structuralism, the atheistic ideas of the post-Enlightment, . . . a new anthropology that is based on something genuinely Christian."[2]

The Christian anthropology of John Paul II is fully presented in his

---

1. P. Gray, "Empire of the Spirit." *Time* 144, no. 26 (1994), 54.
2. Papal spokesman Joaquin Navarro-Valls, quoted in J. Elson, "Man of the Year," idem, 65.

encyclicals, letters, and homilies. But the goal of this book is more limited. It is to present and explore Karol Wojtyła's anthropology before 1978 with a view to better understanding and explaining his papal pronouncements. To do this I will present and analyze one of the cornerstones of his theory—the notion of the human person as the efficient cause of his own action.[3]

Chapter 2 provides an introduction to the intellectual biography of Karol Wojtyła . Describing the intellectual and cultural climate of Poland in the years after the Second World War, it traces the beginnings of Wojtyła's anthropological and ethical interests. Also, it analyzes the problem of human efficacy as it appeared in his early works, especially in *On the Possibility of Constructing a Christian Ethics on the Basis of the System of Max Scheler*[4] and *Lublin Lectures.*[5]

The third chapter analyzes the development of Wojtyła's philosophical method. Two main influences on his thought are examined: Thomism and phenomenology. Also, the question of the Christian character of Wojtyła's theory is addressed. The chapter ends with an account of Wojtyła's mature method as presented in his books *Love and Responsibility*[6] and *The Acting Person,*[7] as well as in certain articles published after 1969.

---

3. Throughout this paper, the notion "efficient cause" is used in its Aristotelian sense, as "the primary source of the change or coming to rest" (Aristotle, *Physics* 2.3.30–32).

4. *Ocena możliwości zbudowania etyki chrześcijańskiej przy założeniach systemu Maksa Schelera* (Lublin: Towarzystwo Naukowe Katolickiego Uniwersytetu Lubelskiego, 1959).

5. *Wykłady lubelskie* (Lublin: Wydawnictwo Towarzystwa Naukowego Katolickiego Uniwersytetu Lubelskiego, 1986).

6. *Miłość i odpowiedzialność* (Lublin: Wydawnictwo Towarzystwa Naukowego Katolickiego Uniwersytetu Lubelskiego, 1986). English translation: *Love and Responsibility,* trans. H. T. Willetts (New York: Farrar, Straus, Giroux, 1981).

7. *Osoba i czyn* (Kraków: Polskie Towarzystwo Teologiczne, 1985). English translation: *The Acting Person,* trans. A. Potocki, rev. Anna-Teresa Tymieniecka (Boston: Reidel, 1979).

Chapters 4 and 5 present Wojtyła's mature account of human efficient causality. Chapter 4 discusses Wojtyła's theory of consciousness,
especially the elements that distinguish his theory from that of classical phenomenology. The fifth chapter discusses the two notions that
are fundamental for Wojtyła's account of human action: transcendence and integration. The summarizing chapter presents the author's
own judgment about Wojtyła's theory of human efficacy, some questions about its weaknesses, and possibilities of further development.

To understand Wojtyła's thought it is helpful to review the intellectual biography of the man who would become the first slavic Pope.
Karol Wojtyła was born May 18, 1920, in Wadowice, a small town in
southern Poland, near Cracow. In Wadowice, he attended grammar
and high school. In 1938 Wojtyła began his studies at the Jagiellonian
University in Cracow in the humanities section of the philosophical
faculty. His principal subject was Polish philology. These studies were
interrupted in the fall of 1939 by the beginning of the Second World
War. During the German occupation of Poland, Wojtyła worked in
the chemical factory at Solvay. In those dark years, he wrote his first
dramas: *David* (1939), *Job* (1940), and *Jeremiah* (1940).

Wojtyła was in love with the theater and poetry from a very young
age. As a teenager, he was very active as an actor and director in
Wadowice's high school theater. Some of his earliest poems come
from that time. The poetic cycle known as *Renesansowy Psałterz* (Re-
naissance psalter) includes "White Grave," in memory of his mother,
and "Magnificat," where he calls God "Father of Great Poetry."[8] In
Nazi-occupied Cracow, Wojtyła was engaged in the illegal, underground Rhapsodic Theater. Together with other students and some
professional actors, and risking death in the Auschwitz concentration

---

8. *Poezje i dramaty* (Kraków: Znak, 1979), 261–62. Cf. T. Szulc, *Pope John Paul II: The
Biography* (New York: Scribner, 1995), 96.

camp, he performed in private homes the masterpieces of Polish romantic drama by Juliusz Słowacki, Adam Mickiewicz, and Cyprian Kamil Norwid.

While reading, performing, and meditating upon writings of Polish and European poets, Wojtyła learned to appreciate the greatness, complexity, and depth of the human person. From that time on, the human drama became the center of his work as a philosopher, poet, and priest. It seems that Wojtyła's poetic gift of grasping the essences of observed things naturally prepared and predisposed him for a fruitful encounter with phenomenology.

In October of 1942, Wojtyła, to the great surprise of his colleagues in the theater, entered the underground Catholic seminary in Cracow with the intention of becoming a Catholic priest. He was ordained on November 1, 1946, by Cardinal Adam Sapieha, who shortly after the ordination sent his favorite student for doctoral studies to the Angelicum, the Dominican university in Rome. Wojtyła's doctoral thesis was written under the direction of the Dominican Thomist Reginald Garrigou-Lagrange on the theme of faith in St. John of the Cross: *Questio de fide apud Sanctem Joannem a Cruce.*[9]

The theology and spirituality of St. John of the Cross left a profound mark on the personality of the young Wojtyła. He began reading the texts of the Mystical Doctor in Spanish while he was still in seminary in Cracow. In February of 1946, during a dogmatic theology seminar, he presented a paper, "Analysis of Faith according to St. John of the Cross: Faith as Means of Uniting the Soul with God."[10] Also, because of his fascination with St. John's theology and spirituality, Wojtyła twice tried to join the Carmelite order. In 1942 the provincial

---

9. Szczypka, J. *Jan Paweł II: Rodowód* (Warszawa: Instytut Wydawniczy Pax, 1990), 129.

10. *Kalendarium życia Karola Wojtyły*, red. Adam Boniecki (Kraków: Znak, 1983), 94. Szulc, 132.

of the Polish Carmelites, Father Józef Prus, asked him to wait, since at that time the Carmelites were not accepting any new novices.[11] In 1946, he tried again,shortly before his priestly ordination, but his decision was opposed by Cardinal Sapieha.[12] The strong influence of Carmelite spirituality upon him is visible in his poetry. His "Song of the Hidden God" clearly resembles the "Spiritual Song" of St. John of the Cross.[13] Jan Galarowicz emphasizes the influence of the Mystical Doctor on Wojtyła's anthropology: "As a fruit of his studies on St. John of the Cross, Wojtyła outlined his own adequate anthropology. Its fundamental thesis says that the essence of human existence consists in human interiority. The most important truth about human interiority is its having roots in the source of every being—in God."[14]

Wojtyła passed his doctoral exam at the Angelicum on June 14, 1948. Five days later he defended his S.T.D. dissertation, in both cases obtaining the highest number of points possible. Paradoxically, he could not receive his doctorate at the Angelicum, for a necessary requirement was the publication of the dissertation, which Wojtyła could not afford. After returning to Poland in June 1948, Wojtyła presented, in November 1948, an expanded text of his Angelicum dissertation to the Theological Faculty of the Jagiellonian University in Cracow. After passing the necessary exams, he finally received the Doctorate in Sacred Theology on December 16, 1948.[15]

11. Szczypka, 94.

12. Ibid., 110.

13. Karol Wojtyła, *Collected Poems*, trans. Jerzy Peterkiewicz (New York: Random House, 1979), 24–49; Szulc, 130.

14. Jan Galarowicz, *Człowiek jest osobą. Podstawy antropologii filozoficznej Karola Wojtyły* (Kraków: Wydawnictwo Naukowe Papieskiej Akademii Teologicznej, 1994), 31. Henceforth all English translations of Polish sources are those of the author (J.K.), unless otherwise noted.

15. Szczypka, 134; Szulc, 161.

CHAPTER 2

The Early Writings

ETWEEN JULY 1948 and September 1949, Wojtyła worked as a parish priest in the small village Niegowić south of Cracow. Then he returned to Cracow, where he served for two years as an associate pastor in St. Florian's parish. On September 1, 1951, the new Archbishop of Cracow,[1] Eugeniusz Baziak, ordered Wojtyła to take a two-year sabbatical from any kind of pastoral work in order to write a habilitation thesis.[2] Father Ignacy Różycki, one of Wojtyła's former professors, suggested the topic of the compatibility of the ethical system of the German phenomenologist Max Scheler and revealed Christian ethics.[3]

Max Scheler (1874–1928) was one of the most gifted students of the founder of phenomenology, Edmund Husserl (1858–1938). Husserl's

1. Cardinal Adam Stefan Sapieha, who sent Wojtyła to Rome for his doctoral studies, died on July 23, 1951.

2. In Poland's higher education, habilitation is a process in which a person with a doctoral degree receives a right to lecture at a university level and to direct students in master's, licentiate, and doctoral programs. In order to complete the hablilitation process, a person is required to write and publish a habilitation thesis as well as to defend it during an exam.

3. George H. Williams, *The Mind of John Paul II: Origins of His Thought and Action* (New York: Seabury Press, 1981), 115. Tad Szulc writes that Wojtyła listened to some lectures on Scheler as early as the fall of 1938, during his first year at the Jagiellonian University in Cracow (*Pope John Paul II: The Biography,* 89).

idea was to convert philosophy into the science of the reality studied by the other sciences and therefore the science supreme over the other sciences. Through a disciplined concentration upon given phenomena and a method of criticism and rechecking, a philosopher is to uncover the essences of phenomena, and possibly even their reality. Helpful in this attempt was a method of *epoché*, invented by Husserl, which consists in suspending all philosophical and personal presuppositions at the beginning of the cognitive process in order that the phenomena alone may speak to the person.[4]

Scheler studied at the University of Munich and then taught as a young docent in Jena, and later in Munich. In 1910, he went to Göttingen in order to be close to Husserl.[5] He became one of the editors of Husserl's phenomenological annual, *Das Jahrbuch fur Philosophie und phenomenologische Forschung*. In its first volume (1913) he printed the first part of his famous *Der Formalismus und die materiale Wertethik*,[6] which became the main focus of Wojtyła's habilitation thesis. Scheler was regarded by many Catholic thinkers as a potential ally. Fascinated by Catholic liturgy, he had converted to Catholicism from Judaism as a fourteen-year-old boy. His links with the Catholic Church were strengthened by his second marriage, to Maerit Furt-

4. Williams, 116–19.

5. In addition to Scheler, two other figures important in Wojtyła's biography belonged to Husserl's circle in Göttingen: Edith Stein, canonized by John Paul II in 1998, and Roman Ingarden, later a professor of Jagiellonian University, whom Wojtyła would meet in Cracow (ibid., 120).

6. The second part was published in the 1916 issue. For the general edition of Max Scheler's works see: *Gesamelte Werke*, ed. Maria Scheler (Bern: Francke Verlag, 1954–69) and Manfred S. Frings (Bonn: Bouvier Verlag, 1985–). *Der Formalismus* was published in 1954 in the second volume of this edition; the English translation is *Formalism in Ethics and Non-Formal Ethics of Values: A New Attempt toward the Foundation of an Ethical Personalism*, trans. Manfred S. Frings and Roger L. Funk (Evanston, Ill.: Northwestern University Press, 1973).

waengler, a Catholic, during Advent 1912. The years between 1912 to 1922 are considered by Scheler's biographers as the explicitly Catholic phase in his life, before he turned to pantheism.[7] Under Scheler's influence, several members of the Göttingen Philosophical Society converted to Catholicism.

During the winter of 1915, Scheler stayed at the Benedictine monastery in the Black Forest near Freiburg. During his spiritual retreat, he read works of the Catholic Church historian Johann Adam Möhler (1796–1838): *Symbolism; Patrology;* and *Unity of the Church.* As a result of his meditations, he reentered the sacramental life of the Catholic Church.[8]

In his philosophical texts, Scheler wrote extensively about the spiritual nobility of the priesthood and monastic life, the rehabilitation of virtue, the value of religion, and the role of the Church. Scheler's phenomenology was also warmly welcomed in the Catholic world because of his opposition to Kant. A Harvard historian, George Huntston Williams, writes in his excellent study of Wojtyła's thought:

All Catholic neo-Thomists would have a fundamental disposition to oppose Kant and his reasoned system that denied the possibility of the direct access of the mind to the ontic reality in Aristotelian-Thomist thought and, above all, undermined the objective and therefore binding character of revealed moral instruction. Scheler could, therefore, in the realm of ethics, no less than in epistemology, anthropology, and metaphysics, be regarded as a prestigious ally, even if a backsliding Catholic, in reasserting, by virtue of a new methodological analysis, the moral values of eternal philosophy.[9]

7. Scheler gave four theoretical reasons for his break with the Church, of which the first was "the slow and painful realization that even my anti-scholastic and anti-Thomistic version of Augustianism was really incompatible with the dogmatic philosophy of the Church, . . . for even the ontological validity of the principle of causation, the methods of metaphysics [etc.] are dogmas" (cf. Williams, 123).

8. Ibid., 121–22.

9. Ibid., 124. Manfred Frings points out that Scheler regarded Kant's *Critique of Practical Reason* as the greatest masterpiece ever produced in ethics. At the same time,

In the introduction to his habilitation thesis, Wojtyła writes about two other elements of Scheler's ethics that made it attractive to Catholic thinkers: (1) an emphasis on love, and (2) the importance of the idea of following an ethical example *(die Nachfolge)*.[10] Wojtyła points out that these ideas of Scheler inspired new treatises of Catholic morality: *Die Katolische Sittenlehre: Die Idee der Nachfolge Christi* by Fritz Tillmann,[11] and *Organische Aszese* by Hans Schmidt.[12]

Wojtyła emphasizes that Scheler's theory is not a study of Christian ethics. It is rather "a philosophical system, built according to the principles of phenomenology and axiology, that is to describe and explain all moral facts and ethical problems."[13] Even if Scheler quotes the text of the New Testament, he does not engage in theological analysis of Scriptures, but rather attempts to demonstrate the compatibility of his ethical theory with revealed morality. Wojtyła points out that Christian Revelation is not dependent upon any specific philosophical system. The role of a Catholic thinker, however, consists in presenting and interpreting Revelation by using different philosophical theories and languages.[14]

The goal of Wojtyła's habilitation thesis is to test whether Scheler's philosophical theory can be used to interpret revealed Christian morality. The dissertation is divided into two parts. The first part presents the main principles of Scheler's ethical theory. In the second part, Wojtyła compares some of Scheler's theses with the truths of Christian ethics in order to find a convergence or possible differences. The

---

Kant's "colossus of steel and bronze . . . has distracted philosophy from its path to reach insights into moral values, their order and their ranks, and the norms which rest on them" (Manfred Frings, *Max Scheler: A Concise Introduction into the World of a Great Thinker* [Pittsburgh: Duquesne University Press, 1965], 104). Also, Scheler agreed with Kant's criticism of the teleological and eudaimonistic ethics of Aristotle (cf. ibid., 105).

10. *Ocena*, 6.   11. Düsseldorf, 1939.
12. Paderborn, 1938.   13. *Ocena*, 25.
14. Ibid.

encounter with Scheler's phenomenology shaped Wojtyła's philosophy in a profound way. Since Wojtyła is an extremely consistent
thinker, we will see arguments from the habilitation thesis repeated
many times in his later works, including the papal encyclicals.[15]

THE HABILITATION THESIS

Wojtyła points out that in the New Testament ethical values as well
as the ideal of Christian perfection have a practical character. While
doing good deeds, the human person becomes good. While performing morally wrong actions, the subject becomes morally corrupted. In
biblical thought, the subject is understood as a cause of his actions.[16]

Wojtyła goes on to analyze the practical character of moral values
in Scheler's ethics. For Max Scheler, an ethical experience is always an
experience of value. The ethical experience is also an emotional one—
Scheler says that we do not recognize values in an intellectual way, but
we feel values as the simplest elements of conscious life. And so, it is
impossible to further analyze their inner structure or to define them.
"The proper place for an appearance of a value is a cognitive experi-

15. Professor Schmitz rightly emphasizes that Wojtyła's early writings, especially the
habilitation thesis and *Lublin Lectures,* are underestimated by scholars. Of course, the
problem is that these works are still not available in English (cf. Kenneth L. Schmitz, *At
the Center of the Human Drama: The Philosophical Anthropology of Karol Wojtyła/Pope
John Paul II* [Washington: The Catholic University of America Press, 1993], 41–42).

16. *Ocena,* 62. As a basis for his conclusions, Wojtyła points to the following texts:
Jn 5:29, Rom 13:3–4, 1 Th 5:15, 2 Th 3:13, Jas 4:17, 3 Jn 1:11. In his scriptural analysis,
Wojtyła does not make use of professional scriptural exegesis. This does not falsify his
conclusions but certainly influences the language in which they are formulated. In his
scriptural analysis, Wojtyła uses the language of the Aristotelian-Thomistic tradition,
with such expressions as causality, moral goodness, the person, etc. One has to remember that Wojtyła wrote his second doctorate long before the Second Vatican Council
promoted the contemporary biblical renewal in the Catholic Church. In his later writings, especially in his Wednesday Catecheses on the theology of the body, Wojtyła makes
full use of modern biblical exegesis.

ence. . . . A value becomes an object of an intentional feeling [*odczucie intencjonalne*]. The whole structure of this feeling is directed to a value's disclosure, one may say: to a disclosure of an object in its value aspect."[17] Values are seen by Scheler as goals of human ethical action. When human willingness is directed toward values, Scheler calls this a "realization of willingness" *(urzeczywistnienie chcenia)*. It is not, however, an external realization of a person but only a realization of values in a person's internal emotional life. Further, at that moment the person experiences a new value—right or wrong. Since, according to Scheler, values are always emotionally experienced in a given hierarchy, right appears in the experience of the person when the object of willingness represents a higher value in the hierarchy. Wrong appears when the goal of willingness represents a lower value.

Scheler divides all values into material values *(materiale Werte, wartości przedmiotowe)* and ethical values *(ethische Werte, wartości etyczne)*. Values that stand as goals for intentional acts of a person are material values. Right and wrong are the ethical values. Scheler emphasizes that only the material values should be chosen as a goal of willingness. Ethical values are to be experienced so to speak, accidentally *(auf dem Rücken, przy sposobności)*.

Wojtyła emphasizes that this concept of ethical value is a consequence of Scheler's emotionalism. According to Scheler, values can be experienced only in human emotions. To want an ethical value means, therefore, to want to experience one's own ethical righteousness. Scheler calls this "pharisaism" and consequently rejects it.[18] A person

17. *Ocena,* 67–68. It seems that, in regard to Scheler's theory of values, Wojtyła is in agreement with another expert on Scheler, Professor Manfred Frings (cf. Frings, 103–32).

18. Wojtyła quotes Scheler from his *Wesen und Formen der Symphatie* (Nature and forms of sympathy): "Love to a good as good is wrong in itself; it is necessarily Pharisaism" (*Ocena,* 64, my translation). Cf. also Frings, 70.

must not want to be good but should always choose material values that are as high as possible.

Wojtyła points out a paradox in Scheler's ethics that can be explained only by taking into account his phenomenological assumptions and his emotionalist epistemology. On the one hand, Scheler accepts the principle of ethical personalism, which emphasizes that the perfection of the person forms the goal of all human activity. On the other hand, this perfection should never be a goal of any specific action—this would be morally despicable "Pharisaism." Scheler deliberately avoids the problem of human causality in regard to ethical values, and he does not explain how the human person becomes morally right or morally wrong.[19]

Wojtyła points out that Scheler's description of the transition from a value as an object of an intentional cognitive feeling to a value as a goal of willingness needs clarification. In the act of willing, the subject selects a value that he wants to carry into effect. For Scheler, a necessary element of willing consists in an intellectual representation of a value that the subject selects. This intellectual representation is, however, of only secondary importance for human willing, since in Scheler's system only emotions, not the intellect, can discern the essence of a value. Wojtyła points out that the incidental role of the intellectual representation in Scheler's ethics is critical to his treatment of human causality.

Human efficacy consists in the person's giving a direction to his own acts of willing. This direction is created by values that serve as goals of willing . . . Therefore, the representation of a value should become this element which is distinctive for the moment of human causality. In Scheler's system, the repre-

---

19. Wojtyła will return to Scheler's theory of "moral pharisaism" in *The Acting Person* (cf. below, 116–17).

sentation does not possess this meaning; it has only a secondary importance and it does not direct an act of willing.[20]

In Scheler's ethics, neither an intellectual representation of a value nor an intentional feeling can give direction to an act of willing. Wojtyła continues:

An intentional feeling directed toward a value forms a kind of cognition that originates in the depth of the person's emotional life. The source of this cognition is love in which the subject experiences the values emotionally. According to Scheler's teaching, love has nothing in common with any tendency . . . Willing should be as well clearly separated from love. Everything that originates in love has nothing to do with willing [according to Scheler].[21]

In Scheler's theory, an emotional cognition of a value that occurs in an intentional feeling does not inform an act of willing. For Scheler, in an absolutely passive way, the uninformed will is subjected to the emotionally experienced values. Wojtyła points out that as a result of this understanding, any element of choice or decision disappears from Scheler's account of human action. Since the will's participation in the acts of willing is totally passive, the human person cannot be a cause of his own actions. Also, in Scheler's theory the moral values lose their practical character; one does not know how the person can become morally right or wrong.

Wojtyła finds another confirmation of his criticism of Scheler's anthropology in the theory of human conscience. Wojtyła notes that for Scheler the conscience does not play any significant role in the person's ethical life. According to Scheler, the conscience cannot be the source of moral values, since it is sometimes mistaken. Neither does the conscience perform the cognitive function toward the material or

20. *Ocenu*, 69.
21. Ibid., 70.

moral values, since they can be known only through emotions and not through any intellectual faculty. What is then the role of conscience? Scheler says that the individual will choose his own moral goods from the moral values he encounters, making them part of his own ethical ideal and moral ethos. The moral values that the person chooses as his own are summarized in the conscience. Therefore, the conscience guards and preserves the moral identity of the person and his ethical ideal *(ideales Wertwesen).*[22]

For Scheler, an ethical evaluation of a person's deeds consists in comparing the values actually chosen to the values of the person's ethical ideal. Wojtyła points out that according to Scheler this process always takes place in the person's emotional life, from which the conscience is excluded. In the emotions, the subject experiences his own moral ethos as well as discovering the material values actually chosen. For Wojtyła, Scheler's failure to appreciate and properly describe the conscience's role in the person's moral life is another proof of his failure to express the person's causality regarding moral values.

Wojtyła's thesis becomes clear when one compares Scheler's account of conscience with the one found in the New Testament. He states that for St. Paul the conscience is an "inner conviction about the moral goodness or badness of a specific deed."[23] In other words, Wojtyła writes, the conscience can be understood as a subjective norm of the morality of human deeds. The conscience consists of two dimensions: cognitive and normative. The cognitive act of conscience measures the goodness of a deed. The conscience's normative dimension obliges the subject to act according to the recognized norm. "A

22. Ibid., 75. According to Scheler, the conscience performs mainly a negative function, by criticizing and warning when the person attempts to choose values that contradict his personal ethos.

23. Ibid., 77.

morally good deed is performed always in harmony with the conscience; a morally bad deed is performed against the conscience."[24]

Wojtyła goes on to demonstrate the connection between the normative function of conscience and the subject's causality. In New Testament anthropology, the conscience's conviction about a deed's moral goodness obliges the subject to perform such a deed. The opposite is also true: the conviction about a deed's moral badness forbids the subject to perform it. Therefore, the voice of conscience forms an essential element of the person's causality. Wojtyła concludes his scriptural analysis: "The conscience as a conviction testifies to the practical character of moral values; the conscience as an obligation testifies directly about the causal relation of the person to the good and the bad."[25]

Summarizing his analysis of Scheler's theory of conscience, Wojtyła writes that the phenomenon of conscience *can* be discovered and described by phenomenological analysis of the person's experience. Scheler's analysis failed, not because of his phenomenological approach, but because of his anti-Kantian endeavor to exclude any kind of obligation from ethics. "Scheler attempts to exclude obligation from his ethical system because he wants to eliminate any source

24. Ibid., 78.
25. Ibid. Wojtyła's brief but consistent and mature description of human conscience in his habilitation thesis is strikingly similar to that found in his later works, e.g. *The Acting Person* (chap. 4), and the encyclical *Veritatis Splendor*, 54–64. Szulc rightly points out, "In an encyclical forty years later—in 1993—John Paul II would place the greatest emphasis on the role of conscience in the entire sphere of Christian ethics and decision making by Christians in their lives. And it would be upon this foundation that the pope would launch his vehement campaigns in the 1990s—from his absolute rejection of all means of artificial birth control and abortion to priestly celibacy. An in formed Christian conscience, he would insist, must be the ultimate guide in all such decisions . . . Wojtyła's philosophical contemplations in the 1950s were not a simple exercise in abstraction" (Szulc, 182–83).

of negativism from ethics."[26] For Scheler, an ethical obligation is always associated with a negative value. It is true that sometimes an obligation does consist in a prohibition of a negative value, e.g., "do not steal." Even, however, if the obligation demands the existence of a positive value, as in the commandment "love your neighbor," it points out the present absence of this value. According to the rules of axiology, Scheler writes, an absence of a positive value already is in itself a negative value. Therefore, a demand or an ethical norm presupposes in the person the existence of an attitude hostile to the suggested value. Even when the person is convinced about the moral rightness of a proposed value, a demand or a norm leads naturally to the person's resistance, because of the obligation's negative character. Scheler's solution is, one has to create an ethics without obligation, an ethics of values.

In Scheler's system, the value itself, emotionally experienced in an intentional feeling, directs an act of willing. As we saw earlier, Scheler's account of willingness does not describe the actual causal efficacy of the human person. Wojtyła writes: "The comparative analysis of the act of conscience in the sources of Christian ethics points out that the causal relation of the person to the moral values consists in an experience of obligation . . . Scheler reduces the essence of the person's life to emotions and his moral life to an emotional experience of values while totally eliminating the person's causal efficacy."[27]

Wojtyła repudiates Scheler's thesis about the necessarily negative character of obligation: "If I want to avoid evil, I want some good. Also, if I want a good, it does not mean that I want only to avoid some evil."[28] The will directed by an obligation turns to a good. Wojtyła points out that Scheler attributed to obligation a solely negative character because of his emotional presuppositions. It is true that in the

---

26. *Ocena*, 79.   27. Ibid., 81.
28. Ibid.

emotional life, an obligation is accompanied by an experience of a negative value. Wojtyła writes: "In the emotional life, an obligation appears when one experiences a nonexistence of a positive value that 'should be' or an existence of a negative value that 'should not be.'"[29] Wojtyła points out that the obligation is present in a positive and creative way in the informed acts of will, which also form the foundation of the person's causal efficacy. Scheler was unable to describe this positive meaning of obligation, since he reduces the person to emotions.

Wojtyła goes on to describe the difference between obligation and value in Scheler's theory. According to Scheler, a value by its nature is indifferent to existence. It remains a value apart from whether it really exists or not. On the other hand, an obligation, according to Wojtyła, is directed to the subject's will and demands the existence of a suggested value. Wojtyła writes:

When values are given *als seinsollend,* i.e. as the content of an obligation, they are given as goals of tendencies (willing). These tendencies are to carry them into effect: the values are to pass from an ideal sphere to a real one; they are to receive an existence. This realization of values does not originate in the values themselves since they are indifferent to existence. Values do not convert naturally into obligation.[30]

He points out that an ethical obligation always requires a realization of an experienced value. Since Scheler excludes obligation from his ethics, he is unable to explain the value's realization but rather concentrates his analysis on the subject's emotional experience of values. Scheler's ethics is silent about how values come to existence and the causal character of the person in the process.

Wojtyła indicates that Scheler is critical of obligation because of his assumption that an obligation makes the subject's cognitive experience

29. Ibid., 82
30. Ibid., 83.

of value impossible. Especially when the obligation comes from a source outside of the person, Scheler holds that it makes the subject fulfill a command by a direct influence on his will. Such an action is "blind" and inhuman since it attempts to obey and to fulfill the given command without recognition of an involved value.

Wojtyła points out that Scheler's analysis of command is one-sided. A command does not have to influence directly the will of the other person: "Usually, it is rather an expression of the will of the person issuing an order who wants to inform the other person about a good that has to be realized."[31] Wojtyła's definition of command involves an understanding of a suggested value both on the side of the person issuing the command and on the side of the one obeying it. Such an understanding of command, in contrast with Scheler's understanding, can be applied to the analysis of Christian ethics. Wojtyła notes that in the New Testament, one finds commandments which must be fulfilled as a necessary condition of salvation, e.g., the Ten Commandments. One reads in the Gospel according to Matthew: "Not every one who says to me, 'Lord, Lord,' shall enter the kingdom of heaven, but he who does the will of my Father who is in heaven" (7:21). Wojtyła emphasizes that the commands found in Christian revelation cannot be understood according to Scheler's theory, since they do not eliminate recognition of a suggested value. The will of God is presented in Revelation not as a direct cause of human actions but as the source of the whole moral order. As an example, Wojtyła refers to the nineteenth chapter of Matthew, to which he returns many times in his future reflection and teaching.[32]

31. Ibid., 86.

32. Cf. *To the Youth of the World: Apostolic Letter of Pope John Paul II on the Occasion of International Youth Year* (Washington, D.C.: United States Catholic Conference, 1985); *Veritatis Splendor*, 6–26.

In the conversation with the rich young man (Mt 19:16–22), Jesus Christ does not use a command as defined by Scheler. By using the expression "If you would enter . . . ," Jesus describes the proposed good and waits for the decision of the young man. Jesus does not use his divine power to influence directly the will of the man, but provides a motive for his action. Wojtyła explains:

The presence of a motive does not eliminate an autonomous moral act of the human person but makes it possible. . . . The person has to make his own decision about the personal obligation, i.e. to direct his own will to a realization of a moral good. This act includes a causal relation of the person to the values that his will has to carry into effect. This causal relation requires an experience of obligation.[33]

Wojtyła points out this irreconcilable difference between Christian ethics and Scheler's position that in the ethical life there is no place for either an external command or for the internal command of conscience: "The internal command reveals most fully the efficacy of the human person in relation to the good and the evil. In the internal command, a value becomes an obligation for the person."[34] Summarizing his comparative analysis of obligation, Wojtyła emphasizes that Christian ethics describes the human person as the subject of moral values and the cause of his own actions. Scheler describes only the human person's experience of values in the intentional feelings.

The philosopher from Cracow illustrates once again this essential difference between revealed Christian ethics and Scheler's ethics in his analysis of love. He begins with the hypothesis that the importance of love may be a point of convergence between the two theories. However, in the New Testament, love is often the object of a commandment, e.g.,

33. *Ocena,* 89–90.
34. Ibid., 90.

"A new commandment I give to you, that you love one another" (Jn 13:34). According to Scheler, it is absolutely impossible to command somebody to love. Wojtyła presents Scheler's position: "Love is a spontaneous act, purely internal and emotional. Therefore, it is senseless to try to impose it from outside. The love originates spontaneously in an encounter with a value."[35] Wojtyła refers to his previous criticism of Scheler's opinion that an external command *ex natura* eliminates any possibility of a fully human act. He proved that in fact the contrary is true: an external command leads to the subject's recognition of the suggested value and to the experience of an internal obligation. This internal obligation of conscience moves the human will and makes the person the cause of his own actions.

According to Scheler, love forms a part of an ethical experience only insofar as it is directed to the human person: to others or to its own subject. In such an act the subject experiences the ideal values that create the personal ethos of the individual *(ideales Wertwesen)*. Wojtyła points out that, for Scheler, love has an ethical meaning not because it is directed to a person but because it leads to an experience of the ideal values of the person. "Scheler does not give an answer to the question about the ethical nature of the act of love. As a phenomenologist, he states only that directing love to a person leads to an appearance of ethical values in the experience of the subject of love."[36] He contrasts Scheler's account of love with that of the New Testament:

The sources of Christian revelation describe the ethical essence of the act of love in a different way. Jesus Christ teaches that the love of God expresses itself in keeping the commandments. . . . "If you love me, you will keep my commandments" (Jn 14:15). . . . The emotional and cognitive experience of the ideal of Christ is not sufficient as an expression of love.[37]

---

35. Ibid., 93.   36. Ibid., 94.
37. Ibid.

Wojtyła emphasizes that in Christian revelation love consists in the realization of values and not solely in experiencing them. Since, in Christian ethics, love leads to the realization of the values expressed in the commandments, love also discloses the causal efficacy of the human person through acts of willing. In contrast, Scheler describes love as an emotion which has nothing in common with acts of willing.

Concluding his reflections on love, Wojtyła asks the fundamental question for the future development of his anthropology and ethics: Granting that experience forms an important part of love, does love consist in an experience of values or in an experience of obligation?

Wojtyła's answer points to a synthetic vision that would serve as the cornerstone of his philosophy for the next four decades. Love, says Wojtyła, cannot be reduced to an experience of obligation or a reverence for law, as Immanuel Kant suggests. Certainly, an important dimension of love consists in its relation to values. However, Scheler's pure experience of values does not sufficiently describe the phenomenon of love. Love refers to a realization of values that expresses the causal efficacy of the human person. Wojtyła concludes that an adequate theory of love has to describe the connection between obligation and value. Only a union of these two elements can grasp the essence of love. "In love, these two elements of ethical experience do not eliminate but supplement each other. A deep experience of a value transforms an obligation into a firm and efficient act. On the other hand, a firm and efficient experience of obligation helps to create a profound realization of values in the human experience."[38]

In the closing remarks of his habilitation thesis,[39] Wojtyła attempted

38. Ibid., 97. A few years later, Wojtyła repeats this thesis in the *Lublin Lectures:* "Duty and value, both, are the two important elements of human ethical life. Also, they are both universally known as elements of human ethical experience" (*Wykłady,* 50).

39. *Ocena,* 118–25. An expanded version of his chapter was published by Wojtyła in the journal *Polonia Sacra* under the title "System etyczny Maksa Schelera jako środek do

in two points to answer the question, whether the ethical theory of Max Scheler can be used as an interpretation of revealed Christian ethics. Concluding that Scheler's ethics cannot be used as a means to interpret Christian ethics, he points out that one of the weakest points in Scheler's ethics, which basically undermines his entire theory, is his concept of person. Because of his phenomenological method, Scheler describes the person not as a substance but only as a unity of feelings and different experiences. Therefore, Scheler is not able to explain how human actions originate in the human person and how ethical values depend on the person's efficient causality.[40]

Wojtyła concludes nonetheless that Scheler's ethics can be helpful in an analysis of Christian ethics, because it can help to describe ethical facts in their phenomenal and experiential dimension. Ethical facts form objects of the person's internal experience. Therefore, in order to describe them, one needs a method able to study human experience. The method of psychology is not able to fulfill this task, because *ex principio* it puts aside the normative and axiological phenomena of personal experience. Wojtyła emphasizes that Scheler was right in asserting that the method needed for ethics is the phenomenological method, because it grasps the entire content of human experience, including its ethical dimension. Williams writes:

Scheler himself, against the psychologies of his day, asserted that the proper means for experimental research into ethically lived experiences is not introspection and the psychiatrist's analysis of unconscious, hereditary, environmental, or idiosyncratic psychic drives and rationalizations, but rather the phenomenological approach without presuppositions, which, alone of the

---

opracowania etyki chrześcijańskiej" (The ethical system of Max Scheler as a means to an interpretation of Christian ethics), *Polonia Sacra* 6, no. 4 (1955), 143–61.

40. Three years later, in his *Lublin Lectures,* Wojtyła repeated his criticism of Scheler's anthropology in a precise statement: "According to Scheler, the phenomeno-

disciplines, perhaps, takes up the lived experience of the person in its wholeness and the wholeness of the person himself.[41]

Wojtyła agrees with Scheler that the ethical fact consists primarily in an experience of a value, an experience which is directed intentionally to a value. The phenomenological method, he writes, can be used for an analysis of the Christian ethical experience, which originates in a believer accepting in faith the ethical principles of Christian revelation.

Wojtyła indicates, however, that the usefulness of the phenomenological method in ethics is limited. It can describe the person's experience of ethical values, but it cannot define the objective principle that decides why a human act is morally right or wrong. In order to define this principle, one has to place the ethical values in the objective order of the good. Wojtyła emphasizes that this is possible only through metaphysical analysis. Williams rightly points out:

A Catholic ethicist may be phenomenological in his phenomenology but not a phenomenologist, for a consistent or exclusive phenomenology would impose the postulate that ethical value reveals itself only in the lived experience of the person when he acts in the moral realm.... But a Catholic ethicist may be encouraged to go further with the method than Scheler himself.[42]

By the summer of 1953, Wojtyła's habilitation thesis was completed. On November 30, the faculty of the theological department of Cracow's Jagiellonian University accepted 175 pages of *Ocena* as fulfillment of a

---

logical principles do not allow one to analyze a person as an efficient cause, but only as a unity of acts. Therefore, a person does not realize anything but only feels values which flow through in different directions ... Neither the acts nor the values, however, originate in a person as in an efficient cause. At this point, Scheler's phenomenology loses the whole dynamics of the human person who is, for him, only a passive subject of feelings, and not an active cause of his own actions" (*Wykłady*, 32–33).

41. Williams, 136.
42. Ibid., 138.

requirement for receiving the university degree of a docent. On December 1, Wojtyła presented his lecture, "An Analysis of the Act of Faith in the Light of the Philosophy of Values." It was unanimously accepted by the faculty. Unfortunately, the rector of Jagiellonian University, Tadeusz Marchlewski, in his letter of February 25, 1954, refused to confer the degree upon Wojtyła, making reference to some recent communist government regulations. Marchlewski's action proved to be consistent with the Department of Education's decision several months later to liquidate the Theological Faculty of the Jagiellonian University in Cracow after 550 years of its existence. So, yet again, Wojtyła had fulfilled all academic requirements, but was unable to receive the degree.

The publication of Wojtyła's habilitation thesis in 1959 went almost unnoticed by the Polish press. A young student of Roman Ingarden's, Władysław Stróżewski,[43] wrote a short review of *Ocena* in Cracow's Catholic monthly, *Znak*.[44] Walenty Urmanowicz summarized Wojtyła's thesis in the theological journal for clergy *Ateneum Kapłańskie*.[45] A Marxist philosopher, Józef Keller, attacked *Ocena* in the government-sponsored philosophical monthly, *Studia Filozoficzne*, but in the three pages of his fierce criticism he failed to give even one philosophical reason for this criticism.[46]

43. In the years 1987–93 the Dean of the Philosophy Department at the Jagiellonian University in Cracow.

44. "Książki o etyce" (Books about ethics), *Znak* 2 (1961), 272–75.

45. *Ateneum Kapłańskie*, 3 (1961), 279–84. *Karol Wojtyła w świetle publikacji. Bibliografia* [Citta del Vaticano: Libreria Editrice Vaticana, 1980], 57–58).

46. "Zwodnicze rozwiązanie źle postawionego problemu" (Deceptive solution to a falsely formulated problem), *Studia Filozoficzne* 1 (22) 1961, 201–3. Keller attacked *Ocena* so strongly apparently because it was written by a Catholic priest. He does not argue with Wojtyła's philosophical text, but he uses the occasion to attack Christianity and the Catholic Church in particular. His arguments can be summarized in two points. First, there is no such thing as "Christian ethics," because the New Testament formulates only

LUBLIN LECTURES

When Wojtyła finished his habilitation thesis, he was already well known in Cracow among the Catholic intelligentsia, students, and clergy. He had taught Catholic social thought at Jagiellonian University and at some Catholic diocesan seminaries. He published several articles in Cracow's two influential Catholic journals, the weekly *Tygodnik Powszechny* and the monthly *Znak*.[47] Active in ministering to Cracow's students, he was also very much in demand as a retreat director, spiritual adviser, and lecturer.

While working on his habilitation dissertation, Wojtyła came to know Stefan Swieżawski, the renowned professor of late medieval philosophy who, until 1952, taught at the Catholic University in Lublin (Katolicki Uniwersytet Lubelski, often abbreviated KUL). During a mountain hike in September of 1954, Swieżawski suggested to Wojtyła that he should teach in Lublin.[48] One month later, the dean of the philosophy department of the KUL, Jerzy Kalinowski, formally employed the young priest from Cracow to teach a course, "The History of Ethical Doctrines." In the academic year 1954–55, Wojtyła gave the first (and most important for our present discussion) of his *Lublin Lectures*, "Ethical Act and Ethical Experience." The next year, Wojtyła

---

very general moral admonitions, which are interpreted differently by different Christian denominations. Second, the Catholic Church attempts to monopolize the interpretation of New Testament ethics by using the instruments of dogma and authority in place of reason and research. Reading Keller helps one to see that the strong position of the Communist ideology in Eastern Europe after the Second World War was due more to the brutality of the secret police and the power of the totalitarian state than to the intelligence of Communist thinkers.

47. In 1950 and 1952, Wojtyła also published in *Tygodnik Powszechny* several of his poems under the pen-name Andrzej Jawień (cf. W. Gramatowski and Z. Wilińska).

48. Lublin is a city of about 400,000 inhabitants, located in southeast Poland.

taught a course entitled "Good and Value." In the academic year 1956–57, he taught a course entitled "The Problem of Norm and Happiness."[49]

Before giving any more detailed analysis of the *Lublin Lectures* it may be useful to reflect on the history and peculiarity of the Catholic University in Lublin, which so influenced the personal style and philosophy of Pope John Paul II.[50] Williams describes its unusual beginning:

The Catholic University of Lublin grew out of a Roman Catholic theological academy founded in St. Petersburg in 1914 for the training of priests of the Russian-held Kingdom of Poland and for Catholic parishes elsewhere in the Russian Empire. . . . When the academy was closed by the Soviet government in 1918, some of its instructors resettled with their rather substantial library in Lublin. The Polish episcopate under the presidency of the Apostolic Visitor/Nuncio to Poland, Monsignor Achille Ratti (later Pius XI), established it as a university, 27 July 1918 . . .[51]

The first rector of the university, Rev. Idzi Radziszewski, secured the transfer of the rights and privileges from St. Petersburg to Lublin and drew upon the model of the University of Louvain for new statutes. The university opened on December 8, 1919, with five faculties: letters, philosophy, civil law, canon law, and theology. In 1920 the university was accorded recognition as a Catholic institution of higher learning by the Holy See. As a Pontifical University, it is thus of the same age as John Paul II.

On June 29, 1992, at the celebration of the 75th anniversary of

---

49. Wojtyła did not intend his "Lublin lectures" to be published. The German version of *Lublin Lectures* appeared in 1981 (*Lubliner Vorlesungen* [Stuttgart: Seewald Verlag]). The Polish text was published in 1986 (*Wykłady lubelskie*). Both versions consist of Wojtyła's personal notes and synopses prepared for the classes.

50. John Paul II still formally holds a chair in the department of Christian philosophy at KUL, meets frequently with its professors and students, and even sometimes serves as a reader of the students' papers (cf. Williams, 145).

51. Ibid., 141–42.

KUL's existence, John Paul II had powerful words of praise and appreciation for Lublin's Catholic University:

In the period of a dramatic confrontation with marxist atheism, the Catholic University of Lublin became a special witness whose influence reached far beyond the borders of Poland, east and west. For many years, in this vast area dominated by the communist system, in this see of totalitarian coercion, the Catholic University was one of a few islands of free, unrestricted search for Truth. Taking as a fundamental the Highest Truth which is God Himself, the Catholic University fought for man, for his truth and dignity, which find their ultimate explanation and surest guarantees only in the Person of Jesus Christ. The University became a powerful sign of contradiction and a witness of Truth when, in the name of a mad ideology, some attempted to reduce faith, religion, and Christianity to a mere epiphenomenon, an illusion, or a lie. In this battle for the soul of the believing nation, the Catholic University of Lublin became a resilient center of evangelization.[52]

When Wojtyła went to teach at Lublin's Catholic University in 1954, its department of philosophy was developing into a new philosophical school known as Lublin Thomism.[53] Besides employing Wojtyła, the

52. Jan Paweł II, "List do Wielkiego Kanclerza KUL abpa Bolesława Pylaka" (Letter to the Grand Chancellor of KUL Abp. Bolesław Pylak) in *Księga Pamiątkowa w 75-o lecie KUL* [Lublin: Redakcja Wydawnictw Katolickiego Uniwersytetu Lubelskiego, 1994], 9–10. In the second part of this letter, John Paul II writes that the dispute about the human person continues after the collapse of Marxist ideology. In a sense, this dispute has become even more acute, since "the methods of the degradation of the human person and of the dignity of human life become today more subtle and, therefore, more dangerous." The Catholic University has to participate in this fight for man by educating the human conscience and making it sensible to fundamental values such as life, good, freedom, truth, love, justice, and solidarity (cf. ibid., 11).

53. Longtime friend of Wojtyła and later also a student in Lublin, Rev. Mieczysław Maliński, writes that in the early 1950s Wojtyła mentioned to him that a new, interesting school of philosophy had arisen at KUL (cf. Mieczysław Maliński, *Pope John Paul II: The Life of Karol Wojtyła* [New York: Seabury Press, 1979], 135). For more information on Lublin's Thomism see Francis J. Lescoe, *Philosophy Serving Contemporary Needs of the Church: The Experience of Poland* [New Britain: Mariel Publications, 1979]; also cf. Williams, 144–51.

energetic dean of the philosophy department, Jerzy Kalinowski, also hired a young and promising Dominican, Mieczysław Albert Krąpiec. The four Lublin philosophers—historian of philosophy Swieżawski, logician and philosopher of law Kalinowski, ethicist Wojtyła, and metaphysician Krąpiec—became the pillars of Lublin's Thomism. Soon they were joined by two others: methodologist Rev. Stanisław Kamiński and historian of philosophy Rev. Marian Kurdziałek. Swieżawski points out that all six "Founding Fathers" of the Lublin's new school of philosophy shared four philosophical convictions. First, all were convinced that metaphysics had primacy of place in the realm of philosophy. Second, they emphasized the importance of anthropological reflection. Third, they strongly opposed irrational trends in contemporary philosophy. And fourth, they all felt a need for historical analysis of philosophical problems.[54] In the fruitful dialogue of Lublin Thomism, Wojtyła was offered an excellent opportunity to give form to his own anthropological and ethical vision.

Wojtyła's first *Lublin Lecture*, "Ethical Act and Ethical Experience," is fundamental for the development of his theory of human causal efficacy. It consists of three parts, which are devoted to the analysis of three philosophers: Max Scheler, Immanuel Kant and Thomas Aquinas.[55]

Lublin Lectures' analysis of Max Scheler basically repeats Wojtyła's conclusions in the habilitation thesis. Scheler's phenomenological

54. Stefan Swieżawski "Karol Wojtyła na Katolickim Uniwersytecie Lubelskim" (Karol Wojtyła at the Catholic University in Lublin) in: Obecność. Karol Wojtyła w Katolickim Uniwersytecie Lubelskim (Lublin: Redakcja Wydawnictw KUL, 1989), 14–15.

55. Wojtyła summarized the conclusions of his course "Ethical Act and Ethical Experience" in some of his articles: "Problem oderwania przeżycia od aktu w etyce na tle poglądów Kanta i Schelera" (The problem of separating an experience from an act in the ethical theories of Kant and Scheler), *Roczniki Filozoficzne* 5, no. 3 (1957), 113–40; "Zagadnienie woli w analizie aktu etycznego" (The problem of will in the analysis of ethical act), idem, no. 1, 111–35; "Natura ludzka jako podstawa formacji etycznej" (Human nature as fundamental for ethical formation), *Znak* 11, no. 6 (1959), 693–97.

method determined the character of his emotionalist anthropology. For the German philosopher, the person is not a substance but only a unity of feelings and different experiences. Further, human experience cannot say anything about the human subject as an efficient cause of his own actions. Therefore, the person does not realize anything, but only feels the values that flow through in different directions. The main point of Wojtyła's criticism is that Scheler does not explain the universal human experience of being the cause of one's own deeds, and he is therefore not able to present the human person as the source of ethical values. Professor Kenneth L. Schmitz has summarized Wojtyła's argument:

Wojtyła suggests that Scheler employed a methodological reservation that prevented him from acknowledging the experience of the "I" as causal originator of ethical action. The reservation stemmed from several considerations. Scheler presupposed that causality is transcendent, and therefore outside the analysis of experience to which phenomenology is devoted. Scheler's emphasis upon the emotional character of human life emphasized the passivity of the human subject and thereby reduced the active principle—that is to say, the will—to a mere epiphenomenon of the life of feeling within the totality of the ethical act. Moreover, Scheler rejected causal efficacy as part of his rejection of Kant's emphasis upon the performance of duty.[56]

Wojtyła points out that twentieth-century experimental psychology falsifies Scheler's claim that the human person does not experience himself as a cause of his own actions. Some of the representatives of this school emphasize that there is a distinct psychic element that cannot be reduced to anything else and that can be experienced by the human subject as "I will," "I should," or "I must."[57] In this psychic

56. Schmitz, *At the Center,* 45.
57. Wojtyła mentions Narziss Ach, Albert Michotte, Johann Lindworsky, Mieczysław Dybowski, Władysław Mielczarski, and Józef Reutt (cf. *Wykłady,* 35).

element—Ach calls it "the actual moment of the will" *(aktualny mo-ment woli)*—the personal "I" experiences his own efficient causality. Wojtyła quotes Lindworsky: "The act of will consists in this specific experience in which 'I' appears as the cause of activity."[58]

Scheler's ethics of material values was created as a critical response to Immanuel Kant's ethical formalism. Therefore, Wojtyła turns in his analysis to the ethical thought of Kant, especially as expressed in his two monumental works, *Critique of Practical Reason* and *Grounding of the Metaphysics of Morals*. He points out that, as with Scheler, Kant's concept of ethics is a consequence of his theory of human experience. According to Kant, human experience mirrors only the phenomenal dimension of reality, without any access to the "things-in-themselves" *(Ding-an-sich, rzeczy w sobie)*. Therefore, the objects of experience always consist in singular and accidental appearances. Since science is concerned with what is universal and essential, Kant emphasizes, it cannot originate in the experience but only in the subject himself. Both the person's reason *(der Verstand, rozsądek)* and his intellect *(die Vernunft, rozum)* provide some forms—categories and ideas—which bring a unity to the chaos of appearances and serve as a foundation for science.[59]

According to Kant, reason operates with categories, e.g., "substance" or "cause," which merge into the appearances of human experience in order to transform them into the objects of science. The intellect operates with ideas, which do not have any direct influence on experience, but rather define the horizon of the subject's intellectual cognition. Kant mentions three fundamental ideas of the theoretical intellect: soul, world, and God.

58. Ibid.
59. Ibid., 39.

Besides the theoretical function of the intellect, Kant also distinguishes its practical dimension, which directs human actions. In the practical intellect, as in the theoretical one, the singular and accidental data of human experience cannot serve as a foundation for scientific ethics. Further, any presence of *a posteriori* experiential data in the rules of practical reason would mean for Kant an interference of nature in the realm of will. Since, for Kant, nature is deterministic, such data would compromise the freedom of the human will. Therefore, the science of ethics has to be built exclusively on the *a priori* form of the practical intellect, which forms the moral law.[60]

Wojtyła writes that Kant's definition of the human will seems to follow the traditional understanding of the will as a spiritual cause of human activity. For Kant, the will consists in a causal faculty of the human person which can direct the subject to a realization of certain objects. The will is directed in its activity by the practical intellect and, more specifically, by its maxims and imperatives. A maxim *(Maxim, maksyma)* is a subjective principle by which the practical intellect directs the will to a certain object. Wojtyła writes:

If the will directs itself to any object because of pleasure, satisfaction, or happiness that the will expects to find in the object, Kant calls such activity of the will empirical and pathological. Kant takes here a position against any kind of hedonism, Epicureanism, and eudaemonism in ethics. He also eliminates from the human ethical life any emotion that obtains any pleasure or distress from reaching an object.[61]

An imperative consists in a command of practical reason which is not subordinated to a sensory inclination of the subject. Kant distinguishes between hypothetical and categorical imperatives. When a

60. Ibid., 40–41.
61. Ibid., 42.

human person wants to accomplish a certain goal in his life, practical reason chooses the proper means to attain this goal and commands other human powers and abilities to act. This command is called by Kant the "hypothetical imperative" *(hypothetische Imperativ, impera-tyw hipotetyczny)*. The ethical law, however, consists exclusively in categorical imperatives. One can speak about the categorical imperative *(kategorische Imperativ, imperatyw kategoryczny)* when nothing but the moral law, i.e., the *a priori* form of practical reason, directs the will. In that case, according to Kant, the human will is totally liberated from all empirical circumstances and deterministic laws of nature. Wojtyła summarizes Kant's argument: "The moral law is the law of freedom since it originates in the intellect itself, avoids any experience, and belongs totally to the *a priori* order. The moral law, therefore, can serve as a foundation of science."[62]

In the moral law Kant distinguishes between matter and form. Matter consists of different goods which belong to the empirical order and are desired by man, often in a disordered way. He argues that it is not the matter but the form of moral law that should direct the free human will, since only the form is totally *a priori* and originates in practical reason itself. Kant formulates the content of the form of moral law in the following way: "Act only on that maxim through which you can at the same time will that it should become a universal law."[63]

Kant then defines the requirements for a morally good human act. In order for an act to be moral, the person's only motivation must be his desire for conformity with the law. The morally good person acts for no other reason than to conform to the law. When a human deed is performed according to the moral law but under the pressure of

62. Ibid., 44.
63. Ibid., 45.

emotions, pleasure, or other internal or external circumstances, the act is lawful but not yet moral. According to Kant, the experience of duty toward the moral law forms the pure ethical element in human activity. Also, reverence for the law is the only emotion which for Kant is morally valuable. Wojtyła quotes Kant from *Critique of Practical Reason:* "This is the only emotion that one knows totally *a priori* and whose necessity one can understand. . . . The reverence for law is not a motive for morality but morality itself in its subjective dimension."[64]

In his criticism of Kant and Scheler, Wojtyła emphasizes that both philosophers mistakenly presented value and duty as two opposite factors of human ethical life. He, by contrast, reconciles duty and value: "Duty and value, both, are the two important elements of human ethical life. Also, they are both universally known as elements of human ethical experience."[65] Kant and Scheler each detached one element from the ethical experience of the human person and concentrated his whole analysis on it. Scheler reduced the ethical act to singular intentional feelings that are directed to material values. As a result, he created only a psychology of values, which at most can bridge empirical psychology and ethics. He failed to acknowledge the formal dimension of values, which refers to the perfection of the agent and is crucial for understanding why the agent becomes morally good or morally bad while acting.[66]

According to Wojtyła, Kant, with his emphasis on duty, is even further away from a proper description of the ethical act. Kant ignores the *a posteriori* data of human experience and constructs his ethics on *a priori* form of practical reason. As opposed to Scheler, Kant emphasizes only the formal dimension of the ethical act, to the total exclusion of

64. Ibid., 48–49.   65. Ibid., 50.
66. Ibid., 52.

its material dimension. Wojtyła points out that Scheler, despite his mistakes, was much closer to an adequate description of the ethical act because of his emphasis on the human experience. Kant mistakenly thought that a philosopher, in order to create a scientific ethics, must totally abandon experimental data. Interestingly enough, when Wojtyła emphasizes his preference for Scheler's phenomenological method over Kant's rationalism, he clearly lays a foundation for his own philosophical method.[67]

Wojtyła points out that both Kant and Scheler find the essence of the human ethical life in emotions. For Kant, it is the experience of duty and reverence for the law. For Scheler, the ethical life consists of intentional feelings directed to material values. According to Wojtyła, this reduction of the ethical life to emotions is responsible for a strict separation of duty and value in the two respective theories. In order to recognize the compatibility of duty and value, Wojtyła continues, one has first to grasp the true foundation of ethical life, which consists in the experience of being an efficient cause of one's own actions. "An awareness of an ethical value of every deed, and consequently of the value of the human subject, originates in the person's awareness of being an efficient cause of these deeds."[68]

Since the psychological element of the person's efficient causality consists in the will, it is the will to which Wojtyła now turns in his reflections. In the contemporary psychology of the will, he writes, the will is defined as "a specific experience in which the personal 'I' experiences himself as an efficient cause."[69] Wojtyła points out that this

---

67. Maliński writes that Wojtyła's students in Lublin were impressed by his original way of presenting some traditional topics and clearly attributed it to Scheler's influence on their teacher (Maliński, 137).

68. *Wykłady,* 59.

69. Ibid.

school of psychology considers the person's causality a part of personal experience and therefore analyzes it using the methods typical for psychology.

Wojtyła notes that the psychological analysis of the human will was initiated by Narziss Ach,[70] who broke with the typical nineteenth-century psychological conviction that the will does not form a distinct psychic element and should be reduced to an emotion or a sensation. Ach pointed out that the human experience reveals the "actual moment of the will" *(moment aktualny woli)*, which manifests itself as "I really want" *(Ich will wirklich, ja rzeczywiście chcę).*[71]

Ach was followed by others. Albert Michotte described the entire activity of the will, from the appearance of a motive to the moment of decision. In the Polish psychological school, Józef Reutt emphasized in his research that the will is partly qualified by the values that engage the attention of the person. Another Polish scholar, Mieczysław Dybowski, concentrated on the external execution which brings the internal process of the will to completion.

Wojtyła emphasizes that the most interesting idea of contemporary psychology of the will links two aspects of the will: its actual-dynamic moment, and its motive formed by a value. Psychologists of the will also describe duty and value as two complementary elements of the ethical life. Wojtyła summarizes their position: "In the moment when an act of the will makes the efficient determination of the personal 'I' in relation to a value, duty appears *eo ipso* as a constitutive

---

70. Narziss Ach (1871–1946) taught at universities in Berlin and Konigstein. He criticized the associationism school in psychology, which explained the entire human psychic life in terms of associations. Ach and other representatives of *Gestaltpsychologie* held that human consciousness is ordered by certain structures, one of them being the goal of human actions (Cf. *Nowa encyklopedia powszechna PWN*, ed. Barbara Petrozolin-Skowrońska [Warszawa: PWN, 1995], vol. I, 25).

71. *Wykłady*, 60.

element of the experience of the will. . . . Psychologically understood, duty consists in the moment of self-determination of the person."[72]

Kant and Scheler were both mistaken, says Wojtyła, in excluding duty or value from the ethical life of the human person. Both duty and value perform important roles in the ethical life, and what is really needed is a new, synthetic description of the relation between them. His conviction is confirmed by the psychology of the will that places the will at the center of the human ethical experience.

Another significant contribution of the psychology of the will to Wojtyła's own philosophy consists in the notions of determination and self-determination. Both appear for the first time in Wojtyła's writings when he describes the views of the psychologists of the will in his first "Lublin Lecture." Later, both notions will become an integral part of his own philosophical language, playing a crucial role especially in his analysis of human freedom and the relation between freedom and truth.[73]

Wojtyła points to some striking similarities between the modern psychology of the will and the theory of the will of St. Thomas Aquinas.[74] Thomas distinguished two movements (*motio, poruszenie*) of the will, *quoad exercitum* and *quoad specificationem*, which, according to Wojtyła, resemble the two dimensions of the will described by the psychology of the will: its actual-dynamic element, and its motive. In

---

72. Ibid.

73. Cf. *Miłość i odpowiedzialność*, 25–26; *Osoba*, 151–229. See also *Veritatis Splendor* 32–33, though the notions "determination" and "self-determination" do not appear in the encyclical.

74. At a number of occasions, in his early writings, Wojtyła presents the Thomistic concept of the will: cf. *Zagadnienie wiary w dziełach św. Jana od Krzyża* (The problem of faith in the works of St. John of the Cross), 131–38; "O humanizmie św. Jana od Krzyża" (About the humanism of St. John of the Cross), in *Aby Chrystus się nami posługiwał* (Kraków: Znak, 1979), 396; "Znaczenie powinności" (The meaning of duty), ibid., 143–45; "Personalizm tomistyczny" (Thomistic personalism), ibid., 437–38.

Aquinas's theory, the will moves spontaneously *quoad exercitum* because it is directed naturally to any kind of good *(bonum in communi)*. In its striving toward everything that is good, however, the will has to choose a concrete good as the actual goal of its desire. According to Aquinas, it is the intellect that, by presenting to the will representations of different desirable goods, moves the will *quoad specificationem* to a concrete good. Among those goods presented by the intellect, Thomas includes, in contradiction to Kant's theory of maxims, goods of the sensory desires. Since the human person consists of the body-soul unity, the goods of the sensory order also belong to the *bonum in communi* of human nature and serve as legitimate ends of the will.

Wojtyła emphasizes that Aquinas's treatment of the will radically contradicts Kant's theory of the imperatives. Wojtyła writes about Kant:

An imperative originates in the *a priori* content of the practical reason which, in the case of the categorical imperative, forms the moral law. Aware of the content of this law, the practical reason commands the will that in itself does not contribute anything to this act but subordinates itself to the reason and its commands. In this theory, the proper character of will vanishes. Kant speaks about the will's "causality," but this causality does not stand on its own, consisting rather in a subordination to the reason and its *a priori* law.[75]

In his theory, Kant deformed the character of the will by emphasizing only its motives, empirical or *a priori,* while totally neglecting the dynamic character of the will which can be experienced by the subject as "I will." The dynamic character of the will—Aquinas's *motio quoad exercitum*—also disappeared in the ethical theory of Max Scheler, where "willing" is subordinated to the emotional cognition of values. Wojtyła points out that, although Scheler created his ethics in opposition to Kant, his treatment of the will resembles that

75. *Wykłady,* 65.

of Kant. The theory of Thomas Aquinas, on the other hand, keeps a perfect balance between the two dimensions of the will, its actual-dynamic element and its motive.

Wojtyła thus provided the essential connection that was missing in the theories of Kant and Scheler: the connection between ethical values and the causality of the human person. The explanation of this relation, however, remained a task to be accomplished. At this point, Wojtyła seems to leave behind the theories of the two German philosophers in order to develop his own solution to the problem.

Ethical values come to existence because of the causality of the human person, Wojtyła writes. Therefore, in order to understand the nature of ethical values, one has to see them in their relationship to the human will. In clear opposition to Scheler's theory of ethical "Pharisaism," Wojtyła writes:

Ethical value forms an object of the will but in a different way from any other object. The acting person realizes different objects and values outside of his will but he realizes the ethical values acting in his will itself. This value forms a quality of the will. The will itself is good or bad in the ethical sense but everything else, in and outside of the human person, is morally good or bad insofar as it depends on the will . . .[76]

Wojtyła emphasizes that ethical values, by serving as objects of the will, describe primarily the activity of one's will. On the other hand, ethical values also create a new quality of the whole person. It is important to follow closely Wojtyła's own reasoning:

The acting will is the efficient cause of its own acts and through these acts it becomes good or bad in the ethical sense. This means that the ethical value is not a content of the will's action but rather a content of the will's becoming. Becoming refers to the will not in its phenomenal . . . but in its ontological di-

76. Ibid., 67–68.

mension. Becoming refers to the will as to a real being and in the same way it refers to the person whose faculty is the will. Not only the acting will becomes good or bad in the ethical sense but also the whole human person who is the efficient cause of this acting will.[77]

Wojtyła insists that ethical values are the values of the person himself. Therefore, the fundamental problem as far as the structure of the ethical act is concerned is the becoming of the person morally good or morally bad. Wojtyła points out that neither experimental psychology nor any essentialist philosophy is able to explain this problem. What is needed is a theory that is concerned not only with the essences of being but also with real existence. At this moment, Wojtyła once again turns to the ethical system of St. Thomas Aquinas. Professor Schmitz outlines the reasons for Wojtyła's turn to traditional metaphysics:

He finds that Scheler slights action (in favor of experience) precisely because he slights being in its realistic sense (in favor of consciousness). And so, Wojtyła turns to metaphysics—not out of piety towards a venerable tradition—but in order to retrieve the reality of act, and in order to give to act the primary role within the entirety of the ethical life as it is lived and experienced. I venture to say that Wojtyła is not a metaphysician by calling, and that he is challenged immediately by the practical issues of life. Still, he too hungers after the truth of the way things are, and in order to give a more adequate account of the ethical life, this "ethicist of act" calls upon the metaphysics of being and its anthropology to explain how the human person emerges from the passive subject of experiences to a responsible agent of moral actions.[78]

Following Boethius, Thomas defines the human person as "individua substantia rationalis naturae" (individual substance of rational nature).[79] Wojtyła emphasizes that the rational nature of the person

---

77. Ibid., 68.
79. *Wykłady,* 69; Cf. *ST* Ia, q. 29, a. 1.

78. Schmitz, *At the Center,* 44–45.

reveals itself in the human ethical life and especially in the activity of the will. Aquinas defines the will as a rational desire *(appetitus rationalis)* because of its close cooperation with the intellect that presents to the will different goods under the formality of goodness *(sub ratione boni)*.[80] The *ratio boni* is defined by Wojtyła as the truth about a specific good in relation to the activity of the will. For the ethical consideration, Wojtyła writes, the relation between the act of the will and the *ratio boni* is of essential importance. "The will acting in accord with *ratio boni* becomes morally good, while acting in opposition to *ratio boni* it becomes morally bad. The will becoming morally good or morally bad forms the essence of human ethical acts."[81]

Wojtyła has already pointed out that ethical values refer to the will in the will's ontological, and not purely its phenomenal, dimension. In order to be able to describe the ontological structure of the will, Wojtyła employs another tool used by Aquinas in his ethical analysis: the Aristotelian theory of potency and act.

With the help of this metaphysical theory [of potency and act] and using the principle of analogy, the peripatetic-scholastic philosophy explains every change both in the physical and moral order, regarding both material and spiritual beings. Every becoming and change consists in a being's transition from a potency to an act—potency meaning a certain imperfection of a being which is perfected through the act.[82]

The person reveals a certain potentiality in relation to different goods—for example, health or knowledge—but especially to the ethi-

80. Since the intellect presents to the will different goods in the light of their goodness, the will's movement toward good is not determined by any specific object. This argument against ethical determinism, based on the rational nature of the human will, would be expanded by Wojtyła in *Osoba*, 169–84.

81. *Wykłady*, 69–70.

82. Ibid., 70. After the *Lublin Lectures*, the indispensability of the Aristotelian-Thomistic theory of potency and act became a cornerstone of Wojtyła's anthropology. In

cal good that consists in being a good person.[83] This potentiality is actualized through the acts of will because good is the proper object of the will. The actualization of the will, i.e. the transition of the will from its potency to an act, becomes also the actualization of the whole person. Wojtyła forcefully concludes his analysis by stating that this is the essence of the ethical act.

It is difficult to overstate the importance of the *Lublin Lectures* in the development of Wojtyła's own philosophy. While his *Habilitationshrift* was concerned mostly with a sharp criticism of Scheler's moral theory, *Lublin Lectures* also reveals the positive elements of Kant's and Scheler's respective systems, which Wojtyła used as the building blocks of his own theory of the acting person. As Tadeusz Styczeń, a former assistant to Wojtyła at the Catholic University in Lublin, writes, *Lublin Lectures* lets us see Wojtyła as a craftsman in his own scientific workshop and as "the master of those who learn humbly from others."[84]

Wojtyła's early writings, published in the 1950s and early 1960s, are concerned mostly with two areas: (1) anthropology and ethics, and (2) the problems of marriage and family. While most of Wojtyła's anthropological and ethical writings are concerned with the problem of human efficient causality, it is important to indicate at this point that

---

The Acting Person, he writes: "Indeed, we do not seem to have as yet any other conceptions and any other language which would adequately render the dynamic essence of change—of all change whatever occurring in any being—apart from those that we have been endowed with by the philosophy of potency and act. By means of this conception we can grasp and describe precisely any dynamism that occurs in any being. It is to them also that we have to revert when discussing the dynamism proper to man" (*Osoba,* 113; cf. also, ibid., 76).

83. According to Aquinas, the ethical value perfects the human person in the absolute sense (*simpliciter*), while all other values, e.g., physical fitness or knowledge, perfect the person only in some respects (*secundum quid*). These other values can make the person a good sportsman or a good scientist, while only ethical values can make him simply a good person.

84. Cf. Schmitz, *At the Center,* 41.

this problem also appears in Wojtyła's reflections on marriage and family.

In one of his first articles, "Tajemnica i człowiek" (Mystery and man),[85] the thirty-one- year-old Wojtyła, drawing upon the ideas of Nicolai Hartmann, describes the human person as a microcosm. All of the different strata and layers of being present in the universe converge in the person, who reveals physical-material as well as organic, psychic, and spiritual dimensions. "Man has something from a stone and from a star, from a plant and from an animal," Wojtyła writes.[86] All the energies of the human organism, however, concentrate in the highest sphere of the person—the spirit—which also distinguishes man from all other beings in the universe. This anthropological awareness of the different dimensions of the human person will be crucial for Wojtyła's future pastoral reflections on marriage and family.

In his very first article on the topic of marital ethics, "Instynkt, miłość, małżeństwo" (Instinct, love, marriage),[87] Wojtyła profoundly describes the human sexual drive while reflecting on the nature of the virtue of chastity. He observes that the sexual drive plays an important role in building the marital relationship, which consists in mutual belonging *(przynależność)*. This profound spiritual bond finds its bodily expression in the sexual union between a man and a woman. This objective role of the sexual drive often is not realized by the human sexual desires, which naturally look for their own fulfillment, i.e., for obtaining sexual pleasure. Wojtyła points out that the human sexual drives have to be purified, educated, and elevated to the personal level by the virtue of chastity in order to fulfill their objective social role. When the sexual desires are transformed by the virtue of chastity, the

---

85. *Aby Chrystus,* 28–35. Cf. Williams, 114.
86. *Aby Chrystus,* 29.
87. Ibid., 36–50.

human person overcomes their disorder and experiences his own efficient causality in the area of the sexual life.

In his article "Myśli o małżeństwie" (Thoughts about marriage),[88] first published in 1957, Wojtyła reflects again on the personal character of sexual and marital life:

Everybody has to agree that the main problem of marriage consists in the problem of the person. Marriage is in its essence a union of persons and not only a connection of two different natures, male and female, on the basis of their sex-appeal.... In the natures themselves, in their sexual psycho-physical differences, one cannot find a sufficient foundation for love, which forms the beginning and the reason for the existence of marriage. Human love always is an act of a person directed to a person. All the psycho-physical elements of love ... should not obscure its personal character.[89]

In an article from 1960, "Wychowanie miłości" (Education of love),[90] Wojtyła insists that truly human love can be reached only at the end of a long educational process. Often, love is falsely identified with the sensual and emotional aspects that spontaneously happen in the human person.[91] However, the depth of the person engages itself

88. Ibid., 414–24.

89. Ibid., 418. The necessity of characterizing sexual life in the personalist context will return many times in Wojtyła's reflection: cf. "Problem uświadomienia z punktu widzenia teologii" (The problem of sexual awareness from a theological point of view), *Ateneum Kapłańskie* 64, no. 1 (1962), 4; "Zagadnienie katolickiej etyki seksualnej" (The topic of Catholic sexual ethics), *Roczniki Filozoficzne* 13, no. 2 (1965), 8; "Personalizm tomistyczny" (Thomistic personalism), 439; "Problematyka dojrzewania człowieka" (The problem of human maturation), *Nasza Rodzina* 9, no. 2 (1977), 5; "Rodzina jako *communio personarum*" (The family as *communio personarum*), *Ateneum Kapłańskie* 66, no. 3 (1974), 357.

90. *Aby Chrystus*, 88–92.

91. Here, Wojtyła introduces for the first time the distinction that later will become fundamental for his analysis of human agency, the distinction between "happening" (*pati, dzianie się*) and "acting" (*agere, działanie*). The emotions happen in the human person without the conscious cooperation of the human rational faculties, intellect and will, which is a necessary requirement for a fully human action (cf. "Zagadnienie kato-

in a relationship slowly, only after necessary reflection and deliberation. Wojtyła emphasizes that in order to serve a lasting commitment,
the intense but short-lived sexual emotions have to be raised to the
personal level, which activity requires a cooperation of the person's
intellect and will. The sign of true love consists in the personal experience of being an efficient cause of the act of love.

Wojtyła presented his complete theory of human love in the course
"Miłość i odpowiedzialność" (Love and responsibility), which he
taught at the Catholic University in Lublin in the academic year
1957–58.[92] His lectures were published in 1960 under the same title.[93]
During his course, Wojtyła describes brilliantly how the different
strata of the human person reveal their proper structure and dynamism in the act of love, which also becomes the place of their integration.[94] He gives special attention to human sensual desires and emotions that play an important role in the phenomenon of love.

---

lickiej etyki seksualnej," 11; *Osoba*, 109–49). The distinction between *agere* and *pati* was
also foreshadowed by Wojtyła in his description of the different stages of human love in
The Jeweler's Shop (cf. K. Wojtyła, *The Collected Plays and Writings on Theater*, trans.
Bolesław Taborski [Berkeley: University of California Press, 1987], 267–323).

92. *Kalendarium*, 147, 159–60. We find in *Kalendarium* an interesting passage regarding
the beginnings of Wojtyła's book *Love and Responsibility*. In the first half of August 1958, he
was canoeing with a group of students from Cracow on the river Łyna in the northeast of
Poland. One of the participants of this trip recollects that Wojtyła brought with him a
manuscript titled *Love and Responsibility*. He distributed its fragments among students
and they had discussions about it. During that canoeing trip Wojtyła received the news
about being nominated to be an auxiliary bishop of Cracow (cf. *Kalendarium*, 159–60).

93. *Miłości odpowiedzialność* (Lublin: Towarzystwo Naukowe Katolickiego Uniwersytetu Lubelskiego); English translation: *Love and Responsibility*, trans. H. T. Willets
(New York: Farrar, Straus, Giroux, 1981). The impact of this book and its author on the
official teaching of the Catholic Church in the area of sexual ethics after the Second Vatican Council still awaits a keen examination. Paul Johnson points out that Paul VI was
reading *Love and Responsibility* while writing the final draft of the encyclical *Humanae
Vitae* (Paul Johnson, *Pope John Paul II and the Catholic Restoration* [New York: St. Martin Press, 1981], 32–33; Janet Smith, *Humanae Vitae: A Generation Later* [Washington
D.C.: The Catholic University of America Press, 1991], 12).

94. The complete theory of integration is presented by Wojtyła in *Osoba*, 229–96.

According to Wojtyła, the person's sensual desires are directed *ex natura* to the other person's body and its sexual value in an attempt to use the other's body to fulfill one's own sexual needs. Wojtyła insists, however, that the person must never be treated purely as an object to fulfill the needs of others. Human love cannot consist only of sensual attraction and desire.[95]

In his analysis, Wojtyła makes a clear distinction between sensuality and the role played by emotions in the sexual life. According to the young Wojtyła, sexual emotions reveal a special sensitivity to the sexual value of the entire person of the other gender. While sensuality is attracted only to the body of the other sex, emotions react also to other values. Unlike one's sensual desires, which tend to use the other person's body to fulfill one's sexual needs, emotions can contemplate and wonder at the mysterious beauty of femininity or masculinity. Wojtyła points out, however, that the danger of emotional love consists in its possible detachment from reality. The emotional idealization of the beloved often leads later to disillusionment and a painful experience of having been deceived.[96]

Wojtyła underlines that both sensual and emotional attraction play crucial roles in the drama of love. Human love, however, as distinct from a similar phenomenon present in the animal world, must engage the higher, rational faculties of the human person, intellect and will. "Love touches the interiority and the spirit of the human person; as far as it detaches itself from them, it ceases to exist. What is left in the senses and sexual vitality of the human body does not create the essence of love."[97]

---

95. *Miłość*, 94–98 (104–9). Hereafter, the references to the text of *Miłość i odpowiedzialność* will point first to the Polish version and then to the English translation (numbers in parentheses).

96. Ibid., 99–103 (109–14). In Wojtyła's drama *The Jeweler's Shop*, Anna fell victim to this idealization which later resulted in disillusionment (cf. *The Collected Plays*, 267–323).

97. Ibid., 105 (117).

Wojtyła insists that the essence of love consists in an affirmation of the other person as person. First and foremost, love is concerned with the value of the *persona* and not with the changeable values of an individual: beauty, sex appeal, intelligence, etc. Thus, the affirmation of the other person cannot be based solely on the sensual attraction and emotions, but it must originate in the subject's intellect and will. Ultimately, Wojtyła concludes, love is an act of the entire integrated person and consists in mutual belonging and responsibility.[98]

Accordingly, the growth of human love consists in integrating the different processes that are spontaneously happening in the human person, e.g., sensual attraction and sexual emotions, into a conscious act of the whole person that also involves his rational faculties. True love does not just happen in the person but involves an experience of being an efficient cause of the act of love.

Wojtyła's reflections on marriage and family significantly enrich his theory of the acting person. While reflecting on the phenomenon of human love, he faces the complicated world of human emotions and sensual desires that influence so much of the activity of every person. These reflections on the subject of human sexuality, as well as his pastoral ministry among young couples, shape one of his fundamental anthropological convictions—that the human body forms an integral part of the human person. In his writings, Wojtyła has many times repudiated anthropological dualism and emphasized the value of Aristotelian-Thomistic anthropology, which describes the human person as a substantial unity of body and soul.[99]

An impressive characteristic of Wojtyła as a philosopher is his intellectual consistency. One cannot find any sign of a significant change

98. Ibid., 112–20 (125–30).
99. Cf. *Osoba*, 242; *Veritatis Splendor* 47–50; *Evangelium Vitae* 23; "Letter to Families," 19–20.

in his thought during half of the century of his intellectual career. (The same claim cannot be made for many of his contemporaries.) Therefore, the early writings of Wojtyła reveal clearly the direction in which the philosophical reflection of the future Archbishop of Cracow and Pope would go.

CHAPTER 3

The Methodology

As we have seen, Wojtyła's early writings indicate that he was conversant with the history of European philosophy. He knew Plato and Aristotle, was familiar with the Christian philosophy of St. Augustine and St. Thomas Aquinas, and moved knowledgeably among such modern thinkers as David Hume, Jeremy Bentham, Immanuel Kant, and Max Scheler. However, Wojtyła's early work also proves that he reached beyond mere historical exegesis. The young thinker showed an impressive ability to integrate into his own work the thought of other philosophers. For example, in *Lublin Lectures,* Wojtyła borrowed from the twentieth-century psychology of the will, Aquinas's metaphysics, Kant's formal ethics, and the phenomenology of Scheler in order to build his own theory of the efficient causality of the human person.

A question that has to be raised, however, concerns the internal unity of that philosophical construction. Is it a real synthesis of different points of view or just a superficial syncretism lacking any internal principle that integrates different theses into one philosophical system? This question, crucial for an evaluation of Wojtyła's project, has to be approached first by an analysis of his method.

APPROPRIATION OF THOMISM

Karol Wojtyła first encountered Thomism during the course of his studies in the underground Catholic seminary of Krakòw in the years 1942–46.[1] Most of the philosophical and theological courses were taught in the seminary *ad mentem sancti Thomae*, as shown in the record of Wojtyła's exams from the academic year 1945–46: *De Sacramentis de Genere et de Sacramento Eucharistae in Specie, Virtutes Theologicae, Poenitentia, De Deo Uno et Trino*, etc.[2] However, a "Copernican revolution" in Wojtyła's thought occurred in his encounter with Thomistic metaphysics. In the fall of 1942, Kazimierz Kłósak, his director of studies, had Wojtyła read *Ontologia czyli Metafizyka* (Ontology, that is to say metaphysics) by Rev. Kazimierz Weis of Lvov (1865–1934). Forty years later, in a conversation with André Frossard, John Paul II recalled the significance of Weis's book for his intellectual life:

Straightaway I found myself up against an obstacle. My literary training, centered around humanities, had not prepared me at all for the scholastic theses and formulas with which the manual was filled. I had to cut a path through a thick undergrowth of concepts, analyses and axioms without even being able to identify the ground over which I was moving. After two months of hacking through this vegetation I came to a clearing, to the discovery of the deep reasons for what until then I had only lived and felt. When I passed the examination I told the examiner that in my view the new vision of the world which I had acquired in my struggle with that metaphysical manual was more valuable than the mark which I had obtained. I was not exaggerating.

1. In a conversation with his lifelong friend Rev. Mieczysław Maliński, John Paul II said that in his life he had "two great philosophical revelations"—Thomism and Scheler. "St. Thomas gave me answers to many problems, and Scheler taught me a lot about personality and methods of investigation" (Maliński, 159).

2. *Kalendarium*, 85.

What intuition and sensibility until then taught me about the world found solid confirmation.[3]

Wojtyła continued his studies in Thomistic thought in his doctoral program at the Pontifical University of St. Thomas Aquinas in Rome from 1946 to 1948. During those years, remembered as the "Golden Era of the Angelicum," an amazing number of world-renowned professors taught there: Franciscus Ceuppens, Jacques Vosté, Eugenio Toccafondi, Ludwik Bertrand Gillon, Michael Brown, Paul Phillipe, Aloiso Ciappi, and Reginald Garrigou-Lagrange.[4]

While working on his doctoral dissertation, Wojtyła also had an opportunity to study Thomistic theology. Under the direction of a traditional Thomist, the famous Dominican Reginald Garrigou-Lagrange, Wojtyła wrote on the topic of faith in the theology of St. John of the Cross. In the introduction to his S.T.D. thesis, Wojtyła emphasized that the Mystical Doctor had studied at the University of Salamanca during its great Thomistic renewal in the sixteenth century.[5] Hence, the Thomistic terminology in the mystical theology of St. John and, as Wojtyła argues, the absolute agreement in the theology of the two great Doctors of the Church.[6]

---

3. André Frossard. *"Be Not Afraid!": Pope John Paul II Speaks Out on His Life, His Beliefs, and His Inspiring Vision for Humanity* (New York: St. Martin's Press, 1984), 17.

4. *Kalendarium*, 101. The library archives at Belgian College where Wojtyła lived during his stay in Rome provide an interesting insight into the character of his studies. He checked out most frequently the following books: Merkelbach's *Summa Theologiae Moralis* (13 times), Noldin's *Summa Theologiae Moralis* (7 times), Aquinas's *Summa Theologiae*, and manuals written by Voste, Billot, and Pesch. Other books read by Wojtyła: Mercier's *La Vie interieure*, St. Francis de Sales's *Traité de l'amour de Dieu*, St. Bernard's *Opera Omnia*, St. Alphonsus Liguori's *Opere Spirituali*, Origen's *Homilie sur la Génèse*. According to the archives, *La Vie Spirituelle* was the journal most frequently read by Wojtyła (cf. *Kalendarium*, 104–5).

5. *Zagadnienie wiary w dziełach Św. Jana od Krzyża*, 15–16 (18–19).

6. Ibid., 16. A number of neo-Thomists wrote on St. John of the Cross. Cf. R. Garrigou-Lagrange, *Christian Perfection and Contemplation According to St. Thomas Aqui-*

Williams indicates that during his studies in Rome, Wojtyła encountered three major contemporary interpretations of Thomism: traditional, transcendental, and existential. Traditional Thomism was represented at the Angelicum by Reginald Garrigou-Lagrange, who followed the interpretation of Aquinas by Thomas de Vio Cajetan and the Iberian John of St. Thomas. At the Angelicum, or perhaps in the Belgian College, Wojtyła encountered the second interpretation of Thomism, known as "dynamic Thomism" or "transcendental Thomism." This kind of neo-Thomism, which Wojtyła met for the first time through the book by Weis, was connected with Louvain, where the main figures were Désiré Cardinal Mercier at the University and Joseph Maréchal at the Jesuit house of studies. Transcendental Thomism, especially that of Maréchal, arose in response to challenges of Kantian and post-Kantian philosophy. Faced with Kant's impressive claim that the philosopher cannot have any certain knowledge about reality, this neo-Thomism was primarily concerned with epistemology.

The third interpretation of Thomism encountered by Wojtyła was existential Thomism, represented by Etienne Gilson. Gilson's program could be summarized by two postulates: (1) to reconstruct the authentic teaching of St.Thomas Aquinas freed from glosses, commentaries, and historical misinterpretations, and (2) to think about contemporary problems *ad mentem sancti Thomae.* Gilson held that Aquinas's metaphysics was primarily existential, while the traditional Thomism had acquired an essentialist cast under Neoplatonic influence through

nas and St. John of the Cross (London: Herder Book Co., 1937); idem. "Saint Thomas et saint Jean de la Croix," *La Vie Spirituelle,* n. 10 (1930), 16–37; Jacques Maritain, *The Degrees of Knowledge* (New York: Scribner's, 1959), 310–387; Leonard A. McCann, *The Doctrine of the Void as Propounded by St. John of the Cross in His Major Prose Works and as Viewed in the Light of Thomistic Principles* (Toronto: The Basilian Press, 1955); Carlos-Josaphat Pinto de Oliveira, *Contemplation et Liberation: Thomas d'Aquin—Jean de la Croix—Bartolomé de Las Casas* (Paris: Editions du Cerf, 1993).

figures like Cajetan, John Duns Scotus, and Avicenna. The existential
Thomism of Etienne Gilson was introduced into the Catholic University in Lublin by the Dominican Jacek Woroniecki and Professor Stefan Swieżawski. This interpretation of Thomism gained a wide popu-
larity in Lublin and influenced many scholars there, most notably
Mieczysław Albert Krąpiec, O.P.

Wojtyła did not publish anything else while he was writing his doctoral dissertation. Therefore, we do not know his own position in the
neo-Thomistic controversies surrounding the legacy of Aquinas and
the relation of his position to contemporary philosophical problems.
Certainly Wojtyła knew about these debates, since his own director of
studies, Garrigou- Lagrange, played such a significant role in them.[7] He
did, however, reveal his position on the proper interpretation of St.
Thomas in the *Lublin Lectures*. There, he clearly follows the existential
Thomism of Gilson.[8] This can be seen, for example, in the second lecture, "Good and Value," where he begins his account of Aquinas's ethics
by reflecting on St. Thomas's relation to his predecessors. Plato stated
that all beings are good by participation in the idea of the good. Aquinas pointed out that Plato's theory failed to distinguish between the
order of cognition and the order of existence. Therefore, the Athenian
philosopher mistakenly thought that all goods in the universe originate
in the truth. St. Thomas himself accepted the realistic and empirically
based teaching of Aristotle that the goodness of things consists in their
substantial and accidental form. Also, Aristotle's account of the good is
primarily teleological; the good consists in an end of every tendency

7. Garrigou-Lagrange had been at odds both with the historical research of Etienne
Gilson, Marie-Dominic Chenu, and Henri de Lubac, as well as with the transcendental
Thomism of Pierre Rousselot and Joseph Maréchal (cf. Gerald A. McCool, *The Neo-
Thomists* [Milwaukee: Marquette University Press, 1994], 158–59).

8. Cf. Schmitz, *At the Center,* 51.

and desire. "Everything that is desired by a man is a particular good," Plato's disciple writes in the beginning of *Nicomachean Ethics*.[9]

Wojtyła states, however, that there are some deep differences between Aristotle and Aquinas in their theories of the good. Aquinas accepts the Philosopher's teleological approach to good; however, he goes beyond that by emphasizing that every act of existence is a particular good. Wojtyła points out that "in Thomas's theory of the good the existence is prior to the end" and calls his theory "existential."[10] This existential interpretation is present in the whole of Wojtyła's account of Aquinas's ethics. "Perfection is the good all beings naturally tend to. Since perfection consists primarily in actual existence, all beings tend to exist *(actu esse)*; that is proved by the basic fact that every one of them shields itself against destruction."[11] Wojtyła rightly points out that Aquinas linked his existential theory of good with the Neoplatonic theory of participation. Every being is good in so far as it participates in the Creator's pure act of existence, which is the perfect good. "Every act presupposes existence. Existence as the act of essence is the fundamental act of every accidental being. Existence, therefore, is ultimately constitutive for a good. . . . God is pure good since he is pure existence. Every other being is good in so far as it has existence appropriate to its nature."[12]

---

9. *Wykłady,* 95; Cf. Aristotle, *Nicomachean Ethics* 1.6.1096a18−34.

10. *Wykłady,* 142. Timothy Suttor points out that the existentialist character of Aquinas's metaphysics defined his radical originality with respect to Aristotle. Unfortunately, Francisco Suarez, who was "the main channel through which scholasticism came to be known by philosophers of the 17th century and after," had not understood Aquinas's distinction between essence and existence. As a consequence, Aristotle's and Thomas's metaphysical theories were often falsely identified in the last three centuries (cf. Timothy Suttor, "Essence and Existence," in St. Thomas, *Summa Theologiae* [London: Blackfriars, 1964−81], vol. 11, 261).

11. *Wykłady,* 125.

12. Ibid., 174.

Wojtyła's existential interpretation of Aquinas is apparent in his short but brilliant summary, "Good and Evil."[13] It is useful to analyze Aquinas's theory of evil, Wojtyła remarks, in order to understand better his theory of good. "Evil itself cannot exist or act. It exists always in the good as in its subject, and forms a certain lack in it.... [Evil] cannot be a cause or source of any activity, which must always originate ... in a being ... and not in something that does not exist."[14]

Since being always is good, only good can act. Evil can be a cause only *per accidens* when vitiating a certain good activity. Wojtyła points out that St. Thomas's whole ethical theory was created in the light of Dionysius's famous adage from *De Divinis Nominibus: bonum ex integra causa, malum ex quocumque defectu* (complete integrity is required for good, whereas each single defect causes evil). In order to be morally good, a human act must possess all the relevant factors contributing to its goodness. One single defect is enough to make any act bad. However, evil cannot be identified with a simple absence of a good, since, for example, there is nothing wrong in the fact that humans do not possess a strength of a bear. Rather, "evil consists in a lack *(privatio)* of a good that should exist in a particular being because of its nature."[15] Ultimately, good and evil can be understood in Aquinas's theory as *habitus* and *privatio,* possessing and not possessing a particular perfection, *esse* and *non esse.* Wojtyła adds: "It is also impossible for the highest evil, understood as an opposite to the highest good, to exist, since the evil must exist in a good as its subject."[16]

---

13. Several years later, Wojtyła praised Thomas's theory of evil in the article "Problem teorii moralności" (The problem of the theory of morality) in *W nurcie zagadnień posoborowych* (Warszawa: 1969), 226.

14. *Wykłady,* 131.   15. Ibid., 132.
16. Ibid.

According to Wojtyła, the most original and interesting part of Aquinas's treatise about the good is his account of the transcendentals. One can see here a direct consequence of Wojtyła's existential interpretation of Aquinas's ethics. Since the good consists primarily in the existence of substance and its accidents, for an adequate account of the good the most important part must be the analysis of the relationship between existence, good, and truth.

Wojtyła quotes Aquinas: "*Bonum et ens sunt idem secundum rem, sed differunt secundum rationem tantum*" (to be good is really the same thing as to exist, but the words have different meanings).[17] The same thing is simultaneously a being and a good. The essence of good consists in being an object of desire. In order to become an object of desire (Wojtyła comments on St. Thomas), the good must possess a certain perfection, i.e., to be in *esse actu*. Ultimately, Wojtyła concludes, it is the existence that decides the actuality of a being, and the good, in a sense, can be reduced to the being. "*Bonum et ens convertuntur*" (good and being convert).[18]

After the *Lublin Lectures,* Thomistic thought established a significant presence in Wojtyła's philosophy. In *Elementarz etyczny* (Elements of ethics), published originally in Cracow's Catholic weekly *Tygodnik Powszechny* in the years 1957–58, Wojtyła wrote that the assimilation of Aristotelian ethics by St. Thomas Aquinas is an excellent example of Christian striving toward truth.[19] In his essay on nature, "Natura i doskonałość" (Nature and perfection), Wojtyła presented a good summary of the fundamental principles underlying Aquinas's *Prima secundae.*[20] Also, his treatment of natural law closely resem-

---

17. Ibid., 126; cf. *ST* Ia, q. 5, a. 1.
18. *Wykłady,* 127; cf. Thomas Aquinas, *Q. D. De veritate,* q. 21, a. 2.
19. *Aby Chrystus,* 134.
20. Ibid., 146–49.

bled what the Angelic Doctor wrote on this subject in the *Summa Theologiae*'s *Treatise on Law*.[21] Wojtyła's famous *Love and Responsibility* (1960) used Aquinas's thought frequently; for example, Wojtyła's analysis of human sexual desire is based on Thomas's account of *appetitus concupiscibilis* and *passiones animae*.[22] In his essay "Etyka a teologia moralna" (Ethics and moral theology) from 1967, Wojtyła emphasized that Thomism is the best example of applying a philosophical system to an interpretation of Catholic moral teaching.[23] As Thomas has used the philosophy of Aristotle, Christians in every age should use the current philosophies to reveal the richness of Christian thought.

Galarowicz summarizes in four points the most important influences of the Thomistic tradition on Wojtyła.[24] First, Wojtyła learned that *philosophia prima* consists in realistic ontology. Second, Wojtyła learned to trust human experience and human intellect in striving toward truth about reality.[25] Third, Thomas taught the future pope both to reverence the tradition and to be open to contemporary questions. Last, Thomism helped Wojtyła to see the *persona humana* in all its complexity and richness.

However indebted to Thomistic tradition he was, Wojtyła at this point also knew it well enough to suggest some changes and modifications. In *Love and Responsibility*, he indicated that the virtue of chastity should be understood in the light of charity, rather than in reference to

21. Ibid., 147–49; cf. *ST* IaIIae, qq. 90–97.
22. *Miłość*, 132–37 (147–53).
23. *Aby Chrystus*, 463.
24. Galarowicz, 54–56.
25. In his *Wednesday Catecheses* on the theology of the body, John Paul II, following Paul Ricoeur, reflected critically on the influence that the three teachers of suspicion, Karl Marx, Sigmund Freud, and Friedrich Nietzche, have had on the modern culture (*Blessed Are the Pure of Heart*, 168–71).

the virtue of temperance, as Aquinas had understood it.[26] In the article "Problem katolickiej etyki seksualnej" (The problem of Catholic sexual ethics), he wrote that contemporary moral theology should go beyond Aristotelian-Thomistic teleology and emphasize rather the normative dimension of moral theory.[27] In the article "Personalizm tomistyczny" (Thomistic personalism), Wojtyła pointed out that Aquinas's anthropology does not take into consideration the problem of human consciousness, so crucial for modernity.[28] The article "Etyka a teologia moralna" (Ethics and moral theology) calls for a new normative and personalistic interpretation of aretology, which in Aquinas's thought had a teleological and naturalistic character.[29] Both deeply grateful to St. Thomas and critical of some of Aquinas's answers, Wojtyła was well aware that his own philosophy would go beyond Thomism. During his studies in Rome, he wrote to a friend in Poland about St. Thomas: "His entire philosophy is so marvelously beautiful, so delightful, and, at the same time, so uncomplicated. It seems that depth of thought does not require a profusion of words. It is even possible that the fewer words there are the deeper the meaning.... But I still have far to travel before I hit upon my own philosophy. Deo Gratias...."[30]

26. *Miłość*, 150–56 (166–74).

27. *Roczniki Filozoficzne* 13, no. 2 (1965), 5. The phrase "go beyond Aristotelian-Thomistic teleology" has to be properly understood. Certainly, Wojtyła is greatly indebted to Aquinas's theory of human will (cf. chapter 2 of this book). He is more reluctant about the starting point of Aquinas's ethics—his analysis of human action in terms of ends and means (cf. *ST* IaIIae, qq. 1–5)—because of the different emphasis in his moral theory. For Aquinas, a teleological structure of human action has important theological significance, because it allows one to talk about God as *ultimus finis* and *summum bonum*. The main goal of Wojtyła's philosophical theory is to reveal the role that moral norms play in human life.

28. *Aby Chrystus*, 434–36.

29. Ibid., 466–67.

30. George Blazynski, *John Paul II: A Man from Krakow* (London: Weidenfeld and Nicolson, 1979), 57.

APPROPRIATION OF PHENOMENOLOGY

Wojtyła encountered phenomenology for the first time when he was writing his habilitation thesis on Max Scheler. However, two earlier influences prepared him for a fruitful exchange with phenomenology by concentrating his attention on the epistemological importance of human experience: (1) his work on the theology of St. John of the Cross, and (2) his lifelong fascination with literature, drama, and poetry. In one of his first publications, the article "Humanizm św. Jana od Krzyża" (The humanism of St. John of the Cross), Wojtyła emphasized that the greatness of the Mystical Doctor's thought consists in its rootedness in human experience. He wrote: "The principle of insight and experience must form a foundation of every humanism."[31] Galarowicz rightly points out that while working on his S.T.D. thesis, Wojtyła was already a phenomenologist, but without a clear awareness of the phenomenological method.[32]

Wojtyła's poetic gifts also made him more sensitive to the richness and complexity of the interiority of the human person. The autobiographical poem "Pieśń o Bogu ukrytym" (Song of the Hidden God), clearly influenced by Carmelite spirituality, described different revelations of the divine in the poet's own experience.[33] In the poem "Pieśń o blasku wody" (Song of the brightness of water), the poet draws a picture of an internal transformation that occurred in the Samaritan woman during her encounter with Jesus at the well in Sychar.[34] In the poem "Matka" (Mother), Wojtyła wrote about the Virgin Mary's recollection of the moments she spent with her son. In a sacramental way, as the past mingles in them with the present, the memories become reality.[35] In his poem from 1952, "Myśl jest przestrzenią dziwną"

31. *Aby Chrystus*, 388.
33. In *Collected Poems*, 23–49.
35. Ibid., 59–69.

32. Galarowicz, 60.
34. Ibid., 49–60.

(Thought—strange space), which may be called a phenomenological manifesto of the young Wojtyła, the poet, using the biblical image of Jacob struggling with the angel at the stream of Jabbok, writes about his own struggle with imagination and the difficulties of expressing his vision in words:

> Sometimes it happens in conversation: we stand
> facing truth and lack the words,
> have no gesture, no sign;
> and yet—we feel—no word, no gesture
> or sign would convey the whole image
> that we must enter alone and face, like Jacob.[36]

Because of his poetic insights, long before he began to read the works of the modern German phenomenologists Wojtyła knew that all knowledge about the human person must take into account human experience. In the beginning of his habilitation thesis, Wojtyła writes about the starting point of Scheler's ethical theory: "Every scientific knowledge and every science originates in experience. Therefore, an ethics also must begin with experience."[37] Following Scheler, Wojtyła distinguishes experience that can prove useful for ethics from the experience used by empirical sciences and by psychology. Empirical sciences use experience inductively, i.e., gathering empirical data, they proceed to formulate some general laws. Wojtyła observes that when applied to ethics, the inductive method leads only to a sociology of morality. It can describe how people behave in relation to moral norms but it cannot explain the nature of the moral norms themselves.[38] Also,

36. Ibid., 70.
37. *Ocena*, 6.
38. This distinction between sociology of morality and ethics will return in other of Wojtyła's publications, cf. *Elementarz etyczny* (The elements of ethics), in *Aby Chrystus*, 129.

the experience needed for an ethical investigation cannot be identified with psychological introspection, which *ex principio* avoids any moral questions. What is needed for ethics, Wojtyła agrees with Scheler, is a phenomenological method, which vows to describe indiscriminately the whole content of the human experience. With the help of this method one can describe the essence of an ethical fact, i.e., the person's intentional experience of an ethical value.[39]

Wojtyła's study of Scheler's theory taught him a great deal about the merits and the limitations of the phenomenological method. He observes that this method can be much more valuable for ethics and anthropology than Scheler was able to prove. The German thinker was inconsistent in his use of the phenomenological method, Wojtyła argues. Especially on two accounts, in the theory of ethical values and in the theory of conscience, Scheler allowed other presuppositions— among them, his emotionalist anthropology and stern opposition to Kant—to obscure his phenomenological insight. As a consequence, he overlooked two facts essential for his theory and accessible to universal human experience: the fact of human efficient causality and the normative character of the human conscience.[40] The phenomenological method can be used well beyond the limits set by Scheler's paradigms, Wojtyła concludes, in order to reconstruct an original human experience and build an adequate theory of the acting person.[41]

Wojtyła indicates, however, that the usefulness of the phenomenological method for ethics is limited. A phenomenologist can describe the acting person's experience of moral values and the phenomenon of human efficient causality. Nonetheless, since the phenomenological

39. *Ocena*, 7–8.
40. One can find a more detailed account of Scheler's ethics and Wojtyła's criticism in the second chapter of this book.
41. *Ocena*, 124.

method is concerned only with human experience, a phenomenologist cannot describe the essence of moral values or answer these fundamental ethical questions: (1) why one human deed is morally good and the other morally bad, and (2) why the subject becomes morally good or morally bad while performing certain deeds. In order to find answers to these questions, Wojtyła continues, a moral philosopher cannot analyze the ethical values only as a content of human experience but has to place them in an objective order of human goods. In other words, at a certain point in an ethical investigation, one has to abandon phenomenological description in favor of a metaphysical analysis. Therefore, Wojtyła concludes, a moral philosopher can use the phenomenological method to great benefit for his own research, but he himself cannot be a phenomenologist.[42]

When Wojtyła started teaching at the Catholic University in Lublin in the fall of 1954, he already had a clear vision of his own philosophical method. Its fundamental theses were created in a confrontation with Scheler's phenomenology and, therefore, its starting point consisted in human experience. In the *Lublin Lectures,* Wojtyła put this methodological vision to the test of the history of European philosophy by inquiring how different thinkers understood human experience and how this understanding influenced their philosophical conclusions. This is clearly seen in his first *Lublin Lecture,* "Ethical Act and Ethical Experience," where Wojtyła clarified the difference between Scheler's phenomenological method and the phenomenalism of Immanuel Kant.

According to Kant, human experience cannot be a source of any true knowledge about reality, since it is concerned only with phenomena. Phenomena do not carry any information about the essences of

42. Ibid., 125.

things, because while essences are universal and necessary, phenomena always are singular and accidental. Phenomena provide only the matter for human cognition—the form comes from the subject's senses and intellect. As opposed to Kant, then, phenomenologists hold that the human intellect has direct access to the essences of things in a simple insight *(Wesenschau, wejrzenie)*. In this cognitive act, both the person's sensuality and spirituality are intentionally directed to their proper object, the essences.[43]

As opposed to the formalism of Kant, Scheler's phenomenology starts with human experience. However, as Wojtyła proved in his habilitation thesis, Scheler is unable to interpret the whole content of human experience because he rejects metaphysics as a legitimate method of interpretation. It is only through realistic ontology, Wojtyła writes, that the whole content of human experience can be properly understood. Therefore, Wojtyła points to Thomas Aquinas as the master of interpretation of the human ethical experience.[44]

Using integral human experience as a criterion, Wojtyła criticizes in his third *Lublin Lecture,* "Norm and Happiness," the ethical theory of David Hume. The empiricist understanding of experience is largely responsible for Hume's mistakes, Wojtyła indicates. For example, because of this reductionist experience, Hume describes the human intellect not as a part of the whole human being but as an independent subject. Detached from the whole person, especially from the will, the intellect cannot be a source of moral norms, Wojtyła continues. Therefore, Hume takes a quasi-utilitarian position in his ethics and teaches that the maximum amount of pleasure defines moral good.

---

43. *Wykłady,* 23.

44. Ibid., 62–66. Wojtyła points out that Aquinas's account of human will is surprisingly similar to that proposed by contemporary experiential psychology. Both Kant and Scheler failed in their theories of human will (cf. above, 33–34).

Hume's empiricist epistemology, which leads to a false anthropology, is responsible for his failure in ethics, Wojtyła concludes.

As distinct from the habilitation thesis and the *Lublin Lectures*, one cannot find in Wojtyła's book *Love and Responsibility* any methodological analyses. This book presents, however, the first anthropological application of his method, which his two previous books had defined. One can also notice a clear connection between *Love and Responsibility* and Wojtyła's poetic work, especially the drama *Jeweler's Shop*. The philosophy of Wojtyła's book and the poetry of his drama depend upon and explain each other.[45] This indicates once again how much his phenomenological method is indebted to his poetic sensitivity.

Wojtyła's method is consistent throughout the whole of *Love and Responsibility*. The first step consists in grasping the essential elements of the phenomenon and the important relations between them. The second step proceeds further in illuminating the essence of the phenomenon by seeing it in the context of the whole human person and interpersonal relations.[46]

Wojtyła's method can be presented by the example of two sections central for the argument of his book: "The Metaphysical Analysis of Love," and "The Psychological Analysis of Love." In the former section,

45. For example, the first part of the drama describes the growth of love between Theresa and Andrew and its transition from attraction and desire to a goodwill and finally to betrothed love (cf. *The Collected Plays*, 279–93). *Love and Responsibility* presents the philosophical analysis of these different stages of love in its section "The Metaphysical Analysis of Love" (cf. *Miłość*, 69–92 [73–101]).

46. Wojtyła does not clearly separate these two methodological steps. Later, in *The Acting Person*, he argues that the two stages of human cognition, experience and interpretation, penetrate and fulfill each other. Respectively, he holds that a human experience always implies some already existing understanding. Surely, one can again see here Wojtyła's unfolding argument against empiricist epistemology, cf. *Miłość*, 92 (101), 95 (105); *Osoba*, 52–53, 62–64; *Człowiek w polu odpowiedzialności* (Man in the field of responsibility) (Lublin: Instytut Jana Pawła II, 1991), 21, 25.

one finds accurate descriptions of different dimensions of love: attraction, desire, goodwill, sympathy, friendship, and betrothed love. Wojtyła skillfully traces the emotions felt by a woman and a man engaged in a loving relationship; he explores as well the activity of their intellects and wills, the response of their bodies, and future chances and dangers that every specific kind of love presents.[47]

Every one of these is followed by an interpretation based on two main principles: (1) the need for a metaphysical interpretation, and (2) the distinction between *amor complacentiae, amor concupiscentiae,* and *amor benevolentiae.* According to the first principle that clearly emerges from Wojtyła's extensive analyses presented in *Lublin Lectures,* the phenomenon of human love cannot be understood purely on the level of experience. Since love involves the whole human being, body and psyche, emotion, intellect, and will, only the metaphysical analysis can grasp the essence of human love.[48] Regarding the second principle, Wojtyła orders the different sections of the chapter "Metaphysical Analysis of Love" in such a way as to suggest that he accepts Thomas Aquinas's distinction between *amor complacentiae, amor concupiscentiae,* and *amor benevolentiae.*[49] As the following analysis attempts to show, Wojtyła does it out of something more than a reverence for a venerable tradition.

In the section "Psychological Analysis of Love," Wojtyła begins with a description of human sensory and emotional reactions that play a part in a loving encounter between a man and a woman.[50] As this description unfolds, one can notice that it is clearly underlined

---

47. *Miłość,* 69–92 (73–101).
48. Cf. Wojtyła's criticism of Scheler's emotionalist interpretation of love in *Ocena,* 91–98.
49. Cf. *ST* IIaIIae, q. 23, a. 1; Aristotle, *Ethics* 8.3.1156a7.
50. *Miłość,* 92–102 (101–14).

by a very specific anthropology, namely that of the Aristotelian-Thomistic tradition. Wojtyła's phenomenological method does not start in a philosophical vacuum but rather becomes a critical criterion operating within the history of philosophy. Alasdair MacIntyre illuminates this with his distinction between three fundamental ways of conducting a philosophical investigation: encyclopaedia, tradition, and genealogy.[51] According to this division, Wojtyła can be defined as a representative of the "tradition" style of philosophical inquiry.

It seems that there are two main principles according to which Wojtyła draws from the history of philosophy. First, he does not hold to any theory just because of his reverence for tradition. For example, the previous section entitled "Appropiation of Thomism" points out Wojtyła's criticism of Thomistic thought and some of his suggested modifications.[52] The philosopher from Cracow will borrow a theory from the past in order to integrate it into his own system only because he thinks that this specific theory well describes and interprets human experience. Therefore, the phenomenological experience becomes the criterion of an assesment of the history of philosophy.

Secondly, Wojtyła's appropriations of other philosophical theories are always creative. For example, careful reading of *Love and Responsibility* reveals a significant difference between the method employed

51. Encyclopaedists hold that the whole truth is accessible to autonomous human reason, which begins its inquiry by rejecting all the theories of the past and proceeds in the enquiry carefully observing the rules of logic. The representatives of "tradition" believe that every philosopher always is a part of a certain tradition of thought. Therefore, at the beginning of philosophical inquiry it is necessary to reflect on one's debt to one's predecessors, which is embodied, for example, in one's concept of rationality, choice of the questions to answer, and language. For the representatives of "genealogy," rational discourse is only a mask for other endeavors, e.g., a drive to dominate, use, or manipulate others (Alasdair MacIntyre, *Three Rival Versions of Moral Enquiry: Encyclopaedia, Genealogy, and Tradition* [Notre Dame: University of Notre Dame Press, 1990]).

52. Cf. above, 56–57.

by Wojtyła and that of the classical phenomenology of Edmund Husserl. Spiegelberg distinguishes three kinds of reduction in Husserl's method: (1) eidetic reduction (ideation or ideating abstraction), which leads from particulars to universal essences; (2) phenomenological or transcendental reduction *(epoché)*, which consists in a suspension of belief in the actual existence of analyzed phenomena; and (3) philosophical reduction, which adopts a neutral position with regard to all the teachings of past philosophy.[53] It seems that an eidetic reduction is present in Wojtyła's method, its first step identified above as "description." In the first chapter of his *opus magnum, The Acting Person,* which will be analyzed in the following section, Wojtyła calls this first step of his method "induction," clearly in accord with the Aristotelian tradition.

Most certainly, Wojtyła rejects Husserl's phenomenological reduction in the name of human integral experience. According to the Polish philosopher, the analysis of human love must be founded on a realistic vision of the human person and interpersonal relations, which can be provided only by a metaphysical investigation.[54] The analysis of Wojtyła's relation to the history of philosophy also shows that he rejects Husserl's philosophical reduction.

THE MATURE METHOD

The fundamental principles of Wojtyła's method were created in his study and appropriation of Thomas and Scheler. This method was

53. Cf. H. Spiegelberg, *The Phenomenological Movement: A Historical Introduction* (The Hague: Martinus Nijhoff, 1960), 724.

54. Eighteen years later, in the article "Osoba, podmiot i wspólnota" (Person: subject and community), Wojtyła formulates well his argument against epoché, an argument that *implicite* was present in the methodology of *Love and Responsibility*: "In fact, objectivity too pertains to the essence of experience, and for this reason man, the subject, is also given in experience in an objective manner. Experience, so to speak, in the process

put to the test of the history of philosophy in *Lublin Lectures* and applied to the analysis of human love in *Love and Responsibility*. However, Wojtyła presented *explicite* his philosophical method for the first time in the introduction to *The Acting Person*, which opens with this crucial passage:

The inspiration to embark upon this study came from the need to objectivize that great cognitive process which at its origin may be defined as the experience of man; this experience, which man has of himself, is the richest and apparently the most complex of all experiences accessible to him. Man's experience of anything outside of himself is always associated with the experience of himself, and he never experiences anything external without having at the same time the experience of himself.[55]

Wojtyła emphasizes that the experience of man is of special importance for his theory of the acting person. Though there are many ways to obtain this experience, first and foremost, every human being has an experience of man through a subjective experience of himself. Next, every human being experiences the presence of other people. Wojtyła points out that the experience of "I" radically differs from the experience of other people: "The disparity occurs because I am given to myself as my own ego and thus more directly and differently than any other man who is not myself. . . . Everyone is an object of his own unique experience and no external relation to any other human being

---

of human cognition puts aside the conception of 'pure consciousness,' or rather reduces all that it contributed to our knowledge of man to the dimensions of objective reality" (*Roczniki Filozoficzne* 24, no. 2 [1976], 7).

55. *Osoba*, 51 (3). *The Acting Person* is the primary source for this section's analyses. The unfortunate history of its English translation is rather well known (cf. Schmitz, *At the Center*, 58–60). I am using the third Polish edition of *Osoba i czyn*, published in 1994 by Catholic University of Lublin. This edition is basically identical with the 1985 second edition, edited by Andrzej Półtawski in cooperation with the author. The second edition contains a number of significant changes (in about 900 places) in the first Polish edition from 1969, as well as some revisions in the English translation by

can take the place of the experiential relation that the subject has to himself."[56]

The experience of oneself is unique because it is the only experience of man from inside. The primary way of experiencing other people consists in an experience from outside, Wojtyła writes. There are some ways of communicating the human experience of oneself to others but the inner experience itself is untransferable.

Besides the inner experience of oneself and the outer experience of others, Wojtyła mentions two other kinds of experience that contribute to the knowledge of man: (1) every human person has an outer experience of himself, and (2) although it is impossible to experience other people's interior directly, sometimes we know a great deal about their interior experiences, so that "when based on the definite relationship, this knowledge may occasionally develop into something similar to an experience of somebody's else interior."[57]

Summarizing, Wojtyła distinguishes four kinds of experience of man: (1) inner and outer experience of oneself; and (2) outer and inner experience of man other than oneself.[58] Despite the significant differences between those four types of experience, all of them complement and compensate each other while contributing together to

---

Andrzej Potocki edited by Anna-Teresa Tymieniecka in 1979. Those changes include new footnotes, stylistic modifications, new terminology, changes in the structure of the paragraphs, as well as reducing or adding to the text. I will point out some of those changes, as well as the differences between the Polish and English edition, whenever they have significance for my discussion. Hereafter, the references to the text of *Osoba i czyn* will point first to the third Polish edition and then to the English translation of 1979 (numbers in brackets). Also, hereafter, all the translations from *Osoba i czyn* are by Andrzej Potocki unless otherwise noted.

56. *Osoba*, 54 (5–6).

57. Ibid., 56 (7).

58. Cf. Stanisław Grygiel, "Hermeneutyka czynu oraz nowy model świadomości," in *Analecta Cracoviensia* 5–6 (1973–74), 144–47.

the experience and, consequently, the knowledge of man. There remains the methodological question to be answered by Wojtyła: How is it possible to compare the outcome of those different experiences, for are they not speaking in different ways about different objects?

First of all, Wojtyła makes clear that he rejects the phenomenalist or empiricist concept of experience, which he had already criticized in his habilitation thesis and in the *Lublin Lectures*.[59] According to the empiricists, human experience provides the subject only with sense data—phenomena—which are consequently ordered and interpreted by the human intellect. In his article "Problem doświadczenia w etyce" (The problem of experience in ethics), published in 1969 when the first edition of *Osoba i czyn* also appeared, Wojtyła indicates that this empiricist concept of experience is largely responsible for the contemporary crisis in philosophy, which consists in a radical dichotomy between empiricism and apriorism, induction and deduction, experience and understanding.[60] In ethics, this dispersion had an influence on the modern emergence and prevalence of the psychology and sociology of morality, which analyze morality only as an aspect of the person's psychical life or as a manifestation of human social life. This ethical positivism describes the ethical beliefs of individuals and societies but is unable to carry on the perennial conversation that created ethics by reflecting on the fundamental questions: What is morally right and morally wrong and why?

In order to restore the ability of ethics to answer those questions, Wojtyła continues, it is necessary to retrieve an adequate theory of human experience as the starting point of ethics. Therefore, in contrast with the empiricist understanding of human experience, Wojtyła

59. *Ocena*, 7; *Wykłady*, 23–24, 39, 276–79.
60. *Roczniki Filozoficzne* 17, no. 2 (1969), 5–24.

holds that every human experience already includes some under-standing. It is impossible for the human person to experience any-thing on a purely sensory level; the sensory and intellectual cognition constantly penetrate and supplement each other.[61]

Wojtyła points out that human experience consists of a multiplicity of single encounters with reality. From this multiplicity and complex-ity of experiential data, the subject proceeds to grasp their essential sameness in a process of induction. "The transition from the multi-plicity and complexity of 'factual' data to the grasping of their essen-tial sameness, previously defined as the stabilization of the object of experience, is achieved by induction."[62]

Wojtyła emphasizes that the person's experience of himself does not form an unrepeatable and unique experience of this specific indi-vidual that is impenetrable for others. Rather, because the human in-tellect describes the experience of the self using general concepts and compares this specific experience with other experiences of man (outer experience of oneself, outer and inner experience of others), the experience of self becomes an experience of man. This inductive process, in which a multiplicity of single experiences of the self creates an experience of man, is called by Wojtyła "the stabilization of the object of experience" *(stabilizacja przedmiotu doświadczenia).*

He distinguishes two kinds of stabilization: (1) by individuals, and (2) by species. The former kind is proper for the sensory cognition of

---

61. Ibid., 10–15; *Osoba*, 52 (3–4); *Człowiek*, 21–30. Wojtyła's criticism of empiricist epistemology is strikingly similar to that presented by Jacques Maritain in his article "The Cultural Impact of Empiricism," in *From an Abundant Spring* (New York: Kenedy & Sons, 1952), 448–67. Maritain ends his article with this fierce challenge to the American reader, which also helps us to appreciate Wojtyła's epistemology: "In my opinion the War of In-dependence of this country is not yet finished. It will come to an end when the American mind sets itself free from the intellectual heritage of British empiricism" (466).

62. *Osoba*, 62 (14).

animals. For example, due to the stabilization by individuals, a dog or a horse can distinguish its master from a stranger.[63] The latter kind of stabilization, proper for humans because of their rational nature, is accomplished by "mental discrimination and classification." Because of the stabilization by species, Wojtyła writes, every subjective experience of one's self becomes an experience of man in general, which leads to a development of the objective knowledge of man.

The inductive stabilization by species makes possible the "intersubjectivization" of an object. This process is of special importance in the case of the relation, person-action *(osoba-czyn)*, which for every human being is first of all an object of a subjective experience. The induction, however, transforms this experience into a problem and a subject for theoretical reflection. In other words, according to Wojtyła, induction consists in a "theoretical treatment of praxis" *(uteoretycznienie praxis)*.[64]

Wojtyła indicates that his understanding of induction, as defined by the process of stabilization by species, is fundamentally identical with that of Aristotle and contrary to that of the empiricist and positivist

63. Wojtyła does not provide any further explanation of his theory of the stabilization by individuals. It seems that Maritain, from the point of view of Thomistic epistemology, further elucidates Wojtyła's thought: "Thanks to the association of particular images and recollections, a dog reacts in a similar manner to the similar particular impressions his eyes or his nose receive from this thing we call a piece of sugar or this thing we call an intruder; he does not know what sugar is or what intruder is. He plays, he lives in his affective and motor functions, or rather he is put into motion by the similarities that exist between things of the same kind; he does not see the similarity, the common features as such. What is lacking is the flash of intelligibility; he has no ear for the intelligible meaning. He has not the idea or the concept of the thing he knows, that is, from which he receives sensory impressions; his knowledge remains immersed in the subjectivity of his own feelings" (Maritain, 454).

64. *Osoba*, 64–65 (16–17). Wojtyła emphasizes that the stabilization by species does not provide any evidence for human knowledge *a priori*. Rather, it points to the indispensable role played by the human intellect in every single experience.

schools. For Aristotle, "induction consists in grasping mentally the unity of meaning from among the multiplicity and complexity of phenomena."[65] For the modern positivists, e.g., J. S. Mill, induction consists in a form of argumentation or reasoning which deals with the experiential data provided by human senses. While the empiricists apply inductively some general concepts to new objects, the induction of Aristotle and of Wojtyła grasps directly the essences of experienced objects.[66]

Wojtyła also holds that his understanding of induction as a transition from a multiplicity of experiential data to a unity of meaning can be reconciled with phenomenological epistemology. Primarily, phenomenology is concerned with the *a priori* intuitive cognition of what is essential, but, Wojtyła writes, even the phenomenological insight must begin somehow with individuals and work its way toward more general notions. After all, the phenomenological movement was created in a critical reaction to the empiricist understanding of induction and as an attempt to retrieve and deepen the traditional meaning of the inductive process.[67]

According to Wojtyła, induction is to be followed by reduction *(redukcja, reducere)*, which is to retrieve what is irreducibly given in an experience.[68] Reduction, as opposed to reductionism, attempts to ex-

---

65. Ibid., 62–63 (14).

66. "Problem doświadczenia w etyce," 20.

67. *Osoba*, 62 (14). Galarowicz points out that induction in Wojtyła's theory can be identified with phenomenological eidetic cognition. In order to clearly separate his own position from that of phenomenological essentialism, Wojtyła does not use this latter term (Galarowicz, 115–16). Nonetheless, Wojtyła still was falsely accused of essentialism by some Polish neo-Thomists (cf. Mieczysław Gogacz, "Hermeneutyka osoby i czynu: Recenzja książki Księdza Kardynała Karola Wojtyły *Osoba i czyn*," *Analecta Cracoviensia*, vol. 5–6, 1973–74, 133–34).

68. Edmund Husserl's three meanings of reduction were previously distinguished (cf. 66 above). Wojtyła gives to this term a new, original meaning.

plain and interpret by revealing the most fundamental principles of an experienced object.

> When reasoning and explaining we advance step by step to trace the object that is given us in experience and which directs our progress by the manner in which it is given. . . . After all, we are not concerned with the abstract but seek to penetrate something that actually exists. The arguments explaining this existence have to correspond to experience. Thus also reduction, and not only induction, is an inherent factor of experience without at the same time ceasing to be, though different from induction, transcendent with respect to it.[69]

Wojtyła emphasizes that reduction should work only with the material provided by human experience. The analyzed object is to be brought "out of the shadow and into full light for the cognizing mind to thoroughly examine and explore."[70] Reduction enlightens and explores human experience by asking questions. Wojtyła emphasizes, however, that these questions themselves should originate in human experience and be defined by that experience. "These questions do not have an *a priori* character but at the same time they transcend a purely descriptive relation to the experienced reality . . . which is typical for any positivist moral philosophy."[71]

According to Wojtyła, the aim of reduction is to produce an intellectual representation of the object which has to be adequate and coincident to the object itself. Reduction does this by grasping all the arguments and items of evidence relevant to the object in their correct proportions. Later in his book, he defines the process of reduction: "By phenomenological reduction we mean an operation leading to the fullest and simultaneously the most essence-centered visualization of a given object."[72]

69. *Osoba*, 65 (17).   70. Ibid., 64 (15–16).
71. *Człowiek*, 28.   72. *Osoba*, 127 (78).

In the introduction to *Osoba i czyn,* Wojtyła returns in a number of places to his definition of experience, a "direct cognitive encounter with objective reality."[73] In the article "Problem doświadczenia w etyce" (The problem of experience in ethics), Wojtyła elaborates further his theory of experience. "The word 'appearance' *[zjawisko]* points to something that appears *[jawi się]* to man in an apprehensive manner. This apprehension of the object seems to be at the heart of the experience."[74]

In human experience, Wojtyła distinguishes two feelings *(poczucia):* the feeling of reality, and the feeling of cognizing. The former informs the subject that something exists independently from him.[75] The latter consists in the subject's cognizing relation to an existing object. The feeling of reality and the feeling of cognizing supplement each other. "In this context, the feeling of cognizing is revealed ultimately as a tendency toward something that objectively and realistically exists, a tendency toward an object, a tendency toward the truth."[76]

Wojtyła unfolds his argument against idealism by emphasizing that the feeling of reality always points to a reality transcendent to the cognition. This transcendent character of the object of cognition forms a necessary condition for the existence of truth. If the reality

73. Ibid., 55 (7).

74. "Problem doświadczenia," 12.

75. It seems that the feeling of reality can be identified with the human act that the representatives of existential Thomism call a "direct existential judgment." The main representative of Lublin's Thomism, Mieczysław Krąpiec, writes: "In existential judgments: 'John exists,' 'Rome is,' we actually affirm the fact of the actual existence of some concrete thing" (*I-Man: An Outline of Philosophical Anthropology* [New Britain: Mariel Publications, 1983], 134). Krąpiec emphasizes that the existential judgment is the most primary act of human cognition in which the existence of a certain being is affirmed before the essence of this being is known.

76. "Problem doświadczenia," 14. Wojtyła's description of the process of human cognition seems to reflect the classic definition of truth: *veritas est adequatio rei et intellectu.*

could be identified with cognition, as the idealists hold, every single act of cognition would be true and the human striving toward truth would be inexplicable. The indispensability of truth is understandable only when existence *(esse)* transcends cognition *(percipi)*. "Cognition must transcend itself, since it is fulfilled not through the truth of its own act [*percipi*] but through the truth of a transcendent object which exists [*esse*] realistically, objectively, and independently from the act of cognition."[77]

In my analysis of *Love and Responsibility* (above, 63–66), I pointed out Wojtyła's philosophical realism, which is also evident in his later works, e.g., *Osoba i czyn*, the article "Problem doświadczenia w etyce," and *Człowiek w polu odpowiedzialności*.[78] Wojtyła does not use Husserl's phenomenological reduction, which consists in a suspension of belief in an object's existence. On the contrary, in Wojtyła's anthropology, the subject seems to be able to distinguish naturally in his experience between what exists and what does not. Wojtyła's epistemological realism places him among such figures in the phenomenological movement as Dietrich von Hildebrand and Edith Stein.[79]

---

77. Ibid.

78. One word of introduction is required to Wojtyła's book *Człowiek w polu odpowiedzialności* (Man in the field of responsibility) (Lublin: Instytut Jana Pawła II, 1991). The aim of *Osoba i czyn* consisted in revealing the human person through an action. Therefore, Wojtyła put the ethical aspect of the human acts "outside of brackets," deciding to concentrate exclusively on anthropology. *Człowiek w polu odpowiedzialności* was planned as a continuation of *Osoba i czyn* and as an analysis of what had been left "outside the brackets," i.e., human morality. The book was devised as the work of two authors, Karol Cardinal Wojtyła and Rev. Tadeusz Styczeń, S.D.S. Wojtyła sent seventy-four pages of the first draft of the book to Styczeń in the summer of 1972. Other obligations prevented Wojtyła from working on the book, and it was not completed until 1978. Although John Paul II gave Styczeń *carte blanche* to finish the book, Lublin's John Paul II Institute decided to published only Wojtyła's first draft.

79. Wojtyła's realism is closely related to his theory of consciousness. Therefore, this analysis will continue in the next chapter of this book.

Wojtyła ends the presentation of his method in the introduction to *Osoba i czyn* with a synthetic vision of an adequate anthropology. He points out that the radical separation between two great currents in the Western philosophy, the philosophy of consciousness and the philosophy of being, originated in the absolutization of one of the two aspects of human experience, the inner experience of self or the outer one. However, since both those aspects enrich our knowledge of man, Wojtyła emphasizes the need to acknowledge their mutual relatedness.

If anybody asks why, then the answer is that this relation lies in the very essence of the experience that is the experience of man. We owe the understanding of man precisely to the interrelation of these two aspects of experience, and this interrelation serves as the basis for us to build on the ground of the experience of man (of "man-acts") our conception of person and action.[80]

The structure of Wojtyła's adequate anthropology, and surely the structure of *Osoba i czyn*, originates in the commitment to interrelate these two aspects of the human person: consciousness and being.

SOME CRITIQUES OF THE METHOD

Wojtyła's methodology is one of the most fervently debated and criticized areas of his philosophy. On December 16, 1970, the Polish Catholic Philosophical Association organized a discussion on *Osoba i czyn* at the Catholic University in Lublin with Cardinal Wojtyła in attendance. Interestingly, during this one-day conference that gathered Polish philosophers from different schools and orientations, Wojtyła's method became the main topic of discussion. A closer look at this debate, which is possibly the most substantive debate to date on this topic, can help us to identify his method's weak and strong points.[81]

80. *Osoba*, 67 (19).
81. Cf., Williams, 196–97.

Most of the neo-Thomists participating in the conference pointed out that Wojtyła's theory does not have a philosophical character. The rector of Catholic University of Lublin, Mieczysław Albert Krąpiec, defined philosophical anthropology as a "theory of man that makes the human being non-contradictory in the context of its fundamental operations."[82] Therefore, Krąpiec argued, since Wojtyła does not present an analysis of man in all the essential aspects of his life, he does not create a philosophical anthropology but rather an "aspect anthropology" that presents the person only as a subject of morality.

Krąpiec's critical remarks were followed by those of Stanisław Kamiński, a professor of logic and methodology from KUL, and Jerzy Kalinowski of the Catholic University of Louvain. Kamiński held that Wojtyła's method leads only to an analytical description of the subject. This description can serve as a hypothesis, but it cannot replace a philosophical explanation. According to Kamiński, the explanation should consist of logical reasoning that links the presented hypothesis with other theoretical and observational statements.[83] Kamiński's criticism was echoed by Kalinowski. He pointed out that since only metaphysics is able to provide an ultimate explanation of the facts observed by Wojtyła, *Osoba i czyn* does not have a philosophical character, because it lacks a sufficient metaphysical analysis.[84]

Some other scholars participating in the conference defended the philosophical character of Wojtyła's theory. A philosopher of religion from Cracow, Marian Jaworski, wrote that the philosophical anthropology of Wojtyła aims to reveal through the explication of human experience the categories that are proper to the human being.

---

82. "Książka kardynała Karola Wojtyły monografią osoby jako podmiotu moralności," *Analecta Cracoviensia* 5–6 (1973–74), 57.

83. "Jak filozofować o człowieku?" in ibid., 78.

84. "Metafizyka i fenomenologia osoby ludzkiej. Pytania wywołane przez *Osobę i czyn*," in ibid., 69.

This concept of philosophy is a continuation of the tradition of Aristotle, Aquinas, and Etienne Gilson. For Aristotle and Aquinas, a philosophical reflection where the sensory cognition of a being is involved does not directly build a metaphysics but rather a philosophy of nature *(scientia naturalis)*. For example, it is *scientia naturalis* that analyzes the soul as the form of the body. Jaworski quotes Gilson: "One cannot deduce anthropology from metaphysics. Like other creatures, man is an essence made alive by an act of existence, but his nature cannot be recognized apart from this act."[85] Jaworski emphasized that Wojtyła is right when he begins his anthropology by retrieving from human experience the fundamental elements that constitute the human being. Also, Wojtyła's anthropology does not reject a metaphysical interpretation, although Wojtyła himself does not pursue this path in a systematic way.

Wojtyła's assistant from the Catholic University of Lublin, Tadeusz Styczeń, also argued in favor of the philosophical character of his professor's theory of the acting person. According to Styczeń, Wojtyła describes different human dynamisms in order to reveal the character of their source, the human agent. This pointing to the source of all human activities does not provide mere hypotheses, as Professor Kamiński suggested. It is rather a discovery of some necessary principles or causes whose negation would lead to a negation of some basic facts found in human experience. For example, Styczeń continued, the negation of the transcendence of the human person would lead to a negation of all the human acts which may be described by the formula: "I can but I do not have to."[86]

85. "Koncepcja antropologii filozoficznej w ujęciu kardynała Karola Wojtyły. Próba odczytania w oparciu o studium *Osoba i czyn*," in ibid., 97.

86. "Metoda antropologii filozoficznej w *Osobie i czynie* kardynała Karola Wojtyły," in ibid., 111–13. Wojtyła's theory of the transcendence of the human person will be presented in the fifth chapter of this study.

In his remarks ending the conference, Cardinal Wojtyła pointed out that Jaworski and Styczeń understood well the philosophical method of *Osoba i czyn*. In particular, Jaworski was right when he emphasized Wojtyła's effort to talk about the human person in words that are proper to the human phenomenon. Styczeń had explained well the essence of reduction in Wojtyła's method.[87]

The debate over the philosophical character of Wojtyła's theory also touched on his description of the relation between experience and interpretation. Some of the participants, such as Kamiński, criticized Wojtyła's broad definition of experience according to which every human experience already includes some understanding. Cardinal Wojtyła responded to this criticism by saying that *Osoba i czyn* never identified experience with understanding, and that it tried at the same time to point out the experiential origins both of metaphysics and of philosophical anthropology.[88]

During the conference, Stanisław Grygiel pointed to an incoherence in Wojtyła's understanding of induction. According to Aristotle, any inductive generalization originates in an insight into one or more similar objects, assuming that they are given in homogenous experiences. In Wojtyła's theory, though, Grygiel continued, the experience of oneself and the experience of others are heterogenous. They reveal different aspects of the human person and, therefore, the sum of these experiences transcends what is given in every one of them.[89] Responding to Grygiel, Wojtyła agreed that his method needs further specifications. At the same time, he restated the fundamental unity of these two basic kinds of human experience of man, the experience of oneself and the experience of others. According to Wojtyła, this unity is

---

87. "Słowo końcowe," in ibid., 248–52.
88. Ibid., 247.
89. "Hermeneutyka," in ibid., 144–47.

crucial for his adequate anthropology: "Otherwise, the philosophy of the person would not reflect human experience. *The Acting Person* was written in order to show that it does."[90]

From all of this, it is clear that Wojtyła's method requires further specifications and needs some more precise formulations. At the same time, this philosophical method presents the right approach to the human person, to the phenomenon of human agency, and to human causal efficacy. Wojtyła's method is also more traditional than some of its Thomistic critics are able to see. Wojtyła professes epistemological realism in the tradition of Aristotle and Aquinas. His epistemological theory of the animal stabilization by individuals and the human stabilization by species can be reconciled with Aquinas's understanding of sensory animal cognition and of human rational cognition that occurs through a creation of notions as well as through judgments and reasoning.[91] Wojtyła's theory of induction points to the fact, accepted by Aristotelian-Thomistic epistemology, that human cognition starts with individuals and works its way toward general notions and laws. His theory of reduction consists in a process of discovering principles that constitute the analyzed object.

From a methodological point of view, Wojtyła's attempt to build a synthesis of classical metaphysical anthropology and modern phenomenology of the human person is far from complete. His success, however, consists in identifying some necessary conditions on which such a synthesis should be built. First, the starting point of anthropological and ethical analyses always should consist in human experience. Also, in their interpretations, they should be faithful to the content of experience. Second, human cognition does not consist exclusively in

90. "Słowo," in ibid., 251.
91. Cf. Krąpiec, *I-Man*, 120–157.

sensory data that the intellect organizes according to some *a priori* forms and categories. Contrary to the empiricist position, the human intellect participates in every human experience and is able to grasp the essences of the analyzed objects. Third, an adequate anthropology should analyze the real human person and, therefore, should begin with a realistic epistemology. Wojtyła rejects Husserl's phenomenological reduction *(epoché)* as a procedure which deforms authentic human experience. Fourth, an adequate anthropology has to include a description and an analysis of the inner experience of the human person as well as the phenomenon of human consciousness. A theory of human subjectivity is a necessary condition for the objectivity and realism of anthropology. And last, only metaphysics is able to provide some notions and categories that can adequately interpret the content of human experience. In the course of the following chapters, we will see how an application of these methodological principles led Wojtyła to create an adequate theory of the efficient causality of the human person.

THE CHRISTIAN INSPIRATION

The possibility of a Christian philosophy has been, in the twentieth century, the subject of a fierce philosophical debate, initiated by Etienne Gilson. Gilson defined Christian philosophy as "the work of human reason functioning autonomously within the context of divine revelation" and argued that the theories of Augustine and Aquinas are examples of such philosophy.[92] Gilson presented his theory of Christian philosophy on two occasions: in 1931 before the Société Française de Philosophie, and in his Gifford Lectures in Aberdeen

92. Laurence K. Shook, *Etienne Gilson* (Toronto: Pontifical Institute of Mediaeval Studies, 1984), 198.

during 1931 and 1932. Laurence K. Shook summarizes well Gilson's arguments in favor of Christian philosophy:

At the Société debate Gilson employed three basic arguments to demonstrate Christian philosophy. First he maintained that in Christianity there is, over and above practical, speculative elements, a Christian exercise of reason which is not divorced from faith; much is to be gained by turning to "the Bible and the Gospel as sources of philosophic inspiration," especially for pure philosophy and metaphysics. Second, there is an early history of this exercise of reason, especially in Justin, Lactantius, Augustine, and Anselm. And third, this Christian philosophy gives precise expression to the unique understanding of the Supreme Being, the *Ego sum qui sum* of Exodus, thus affirming a metaphysical primacy of being.[93]

Reflecting on Gilson's notion of Christian philosophy, Schmitz points out that every philosopher must draw upon the totality of his sources: social, political, and cultural life, religion, science, art, etc. However, philosophical reflection upon the content of these sources is critical. A philosopher must account for the way he draws upon his sources, since "whatever is claimed for philosophy must be claimed on the basis of the methodological discourse of reason."[94] We will see how Wojtyła created a Christian philosophy of the acting person along the lines defined by Gilson.[95]

Wojtyła's project of creating a Christian philosophy of the human

93. Ibid., 199.
94. Kenneth L. Schmitz, *What Has Clio to Do with Athena? Etienne Gilson: Historian and Philosopher* (Toronto: Pontifical Institute of Mediaeval Studies, 1987), 10.
95. Most of Wojtyła's commentators point out the influence of Christian faith on his philosophy, cf.: Rocco Buttiglione, "Kilka uwag o sposobie czytania *Osoby i czynu*," in: Wojtyła, *Osoba*, 12, 32–42; Galarowicz, 123–26; McCool, 161; Schmitz, *At the Center*, 39–40; Styczeń, in Wojtyła, *Wykłady*, 7–9; Williams, 134–35, 154–204; Woznicki, *A Christian Humanism*, 1–3.

person became clear in some of his earliest publications. Both poetic and philosophical, they are concerned with the problem of human cognition, both natural and supernatural, of oneself and others. In his poem "Song of the Brightness of Water," written in 1950, Wojtyła describes the encounter between Jesus Christ and the Samaritan woman at the well in Sychar.[96] The poem reveals the author's conviction that a natural cognition of man is very difficult, almost impossible.

> But, I tell you, your sight alone
> scarcely catches people as they flow
> on the wave of fluorescent lights.
> They are revealed by what is most concealed
> within them, that which no flame
> will burn out.[97]

Wojtyła writes that the best way to come to know oneself and others is to close one's eyes. Then, one can see everything clearly in the supernatural light of Christ. At the well in Sychar, Wojtyła continues, Christ revealed to the woman the entire truth about herself. This self-cognition was for her very painful but at the same time healing and liberating. Also, this cognition consisted in something more than abstract, intellectual reasoning. This cognition of self was transforming, removing from the woman's heart a heavy burden and bringing it joy and harmony.

It is clear that in the "Song of the Brightness of Water" Wojtyła writes about the transforming power of the grace of Jesus Christ. It is important to notice that grace is not presented by Wojtyła as something external or merely added to human nature. Rather, it is grace

---

96. Cf. John 4:1–42.
97. *Collected Poems*, 51.

that gives to man full cognition of himself and helps him to live according to the full potential of human nature. In this poem, Wojtyła rejects the theory of grace presented in the nineteenth-century manuals of Catholic theology, which was based on a strong distinction between the two ends of man: natural and supernatural. Also, it seems that Wojtyła accepts the theory of grace popularized in the twentieth century by Henri de Lubac in his famous *Surnaturel*.[98] Grace is presented there as the fulfilment of all human natural potentialities.

In his 1957 article "Znaczenie powinności" (The meaning of duty) Wojtyła follows the Thomistic tradition in distinguishing four ways of defining human nature: *natura pura, natura integra, natura lapsa,* and *natura reparata*.[99] Wojtyła emphasizes that the *status naturae purae* is only a hypothetical concept. A pure nature would exist only if God had not elevated human nature to the supernatural order. However, since even Adam and Eve lived in harmony with God, Wojtyła concludes that there has never existed a man possessing only a pure nature. Therefore, every human person who ever lived should be understood in the light of three states: *natura integra, natura lapsa,* and *natura reparata*.[100]

98. *Surnaturel: études historiques* (Paris: Aubier, 1946). Without mentioning his name, Wojtyła constantly refers to de Lubac's understanding of grace, cf. "O humaniźmie św. Jana od Krzyża," "Religijn przeżywanie czystości," "Boże Narodzenie 1958." Wojtyła and de Lubac became friends when they were working together during the Second Vatican Council. For a short but very moving story of their friendship see Henri de Lubac, *At the Service of the Church* (San Francisco: Ignatius Press, 1993), 171–73.

99. *Aby Chrystus*, 142–46.

100. One should notice that this is precisely the method of theological anthropology employed by Wojtyła several years later in *Mężczyzną i niewiastą stworzył ich. Odkupienie ciała a sakramentalność małżeństwa* (Città del Vaticano: Libreria Editrice Vaticana, 1986). The English translation of this book appeared in three separate volumes: *Original Unity of Man and Woman: Catechesis on the Book of Genesis; Blessed Are the Pure of Heart: Catechesis on the Sermon on the Mount and the Writings of St. Paul;* and *Reflections on Humanae Vitae: Conjugal Morality and Spirituality;* all volumes published by Daughters of

Wojtyła continues to examine natural and supernatural self-cognition in his 1950 poem "Mother." The poem describes the Virgin Mary recalling all the moments she has spent with Jesus, in order to discover and experience their deeper sacramental meaning as well as their transforming power.

> There I have returned many a time to memories:
> from which life overflows, surging from within
> with unlikely meaning.[101]

Mary is deeply transformed by every moment she spends with Jesus. Also, thanks to the light given her by the Son, she gains a deeper, supernatural understanding of herself.

> My depths are seen into, I am seen through and through.
> Open to sight I rise, in that vision gently submerge.
> For a long time nobody knew of this;
> I told no one the expression of your eyes.[102]

In his 1951 article "Tajemnica i człowiek" (Mystery and man) Wojtyła reflects on the anthropological significance of Christ's Incarnation. Using the philosophical language of Nicolai Hartmann, he describes man as a microcosm that gathers in itself all the different layers of existence present in the universe: material, organic, psychic, and spiritual. The human person, however, should be understood only in the light of his highest sphere, the spirit. Because of this spiritual

---

St. Paul: Boston, 1980, 1983, and 1984. *Mężczyzną i niewiastą* was written by Cardinal Wojtyła in the late 1970s and was presented as the Pope's Wednesday Catecheses between October 1979 and November 1984. Wojtyła's consistency and intellectual discipline are astonishing, given the fact that he had already defined his method in 1957.

101. *Collected Poems*, 60.

102. Ibid., 67.

dimension, man differs from any other being in the universe and in his spirit he resembles the Creator. Wojtyła points out that the philosophical truth about the human spirit and the dignity of the human person was confirmed and deepened by Christ's Incarnation. "The Mystery of the Incarnation . . . carries in itself the power of turning man to his own human nature. Because of this mystery, man can appreciate his dignity and his proper place in creation."[103]

Wojtyła's early publications reveal a method that he would elaborate and use throughout his whole career. This method rests on an assumption that only the human-divine person of Jesus Christ unfolds the whole truth about man. Therefore, in order to find this truth, one has to look at the human person through Christ. It is important to notice that this Christocentric method was employed during the Second Vatican Council, particularly in the Constitution on the Church in the Modern World, which was written with extensive contributions from Archbishop Wojtyła.[104] One finds in *Gaudium et Spes* (22) a precise formulation of Wojtyła's method:

In fact, it is only in the mystery of the Word incarnate that light is shed on the mystery of humankind. For Adam, the first human being, was a representation of the future, namely of Christ the Lord. It is Christ the last Adam, who fully discloses humankind to itself and unfolds its noble calling by revealing the mystery of the Father and the Father's love. It is not therefore to be wondered at that it is in Christ that the truths stated here find their source and reach their fulfillment.[105]

---

103. *Aby Chrystus*, 31. During the Second Vatican Council, one of Archbishop Wojtyła's most significant interventions referred to the effect that the event of the Incarnation had on all humanity (cf. Williams, 178–81).

104. Cf. Williams, 164–85.

105. *Decrees of the Ecumenical Councils*, ed. by Norman P. Tanner (Washington: Georgetown University Press, 1990), vol. II, 1081. Wojtyła comments on this method in *Sources of Renewal: The Implementation of the Second Vatican Council* (San Francisco: Harper & Row, 1979), 66–84; and *Sign of Contradiction* (New York: The Seabury Press,

It is clear that a consistent use of this Christocentric method belongs to a theology that draws its conclusions from premises known only through faith.[106] However, this method also has significance for a believing philosopher insofar as it changes the way he perceives created reality. One can trace the impact of the Christian faith on Wojtyła's thought through all his philosophical writings.

In the *Lublin Lectures*, Wojtyła incorporated into his own theory some elements taken from Augustine and Aquinas, fully aware that their philosophies were developed originally as integral parts of their theological systems.[107] In *Elementarz etyczny* (Elements of ethics), published in Cracow's Catholic weekly *Tygodnik Powszechny* in the years 1957–58, we see Wojtyła's philosophy developing a dialogue with theology. He makes sure, on the one hand, that his philosophical conclusions are open to further theological reflection, and on the other, that his Christian faith influences the style and direction of his thinking. For example, in the section "Natura i doskonałość" (Nature and perfection), he reflects on the role of perfection in philosophical ethics.[108] Then, he goes on to analyze what changes occur in human ethical action when the agent accepts, in faith, Christian revelation. He emphasizes that man, through faith, participates in the knowledge of God himself,

---

1979), 101–9, 117–19. John Paul II frequently employs the Christocentric method in his encyclicals and papal pronouncements; cf. *Centessimus Annus*, 54–55; *Veritatis Splendor*, 2; *"Letter to Families" for the International Year of the Family*, 4; *Evangelium Vitae*, 29–31; *Tertio Millenio Adveniente*, 4. For a good analysis of John Paul II's Christocentric method see John Saward, *Christ Is the Answer: The Christ-Centered Teaching of Pope John Paul II* (New York: Alba House, 1995).

106. In discussing Christian philosophy, therefore, it is important to preserve the distinction between philosophy and theology. In his introduction to *Lublin Lectures*, Styczeń seems to blur this distinction when he writes that Wojtyła's anthropology, both philosophical and theological, originated in Christology (cf. Styczeń, "Słowo wstępne," in: Wojtyła, *Wykłady*, 9).

107. Cf. *Wykłady*, 123, 141, 174.

108. *Aby Chrystus*, 140–42.

which knowledge describes the order that should exist in the world. Therefore, the intellect enlightened by faith is much better suited to direct human actions. The epistemological position of the human intellect enlightened by Christian faith is described by Wojtyła in the essay "Realizm w etyce" (Realism in ethics) as "supernatural realism."[109]

In *Elements of Ethics,* Wojtyła also reflects on the Christian understanding of grace in a manner that is very similar to the theology of Henri de Lubac. In the section "Właściwa interpretacja nauki o szczęściu" (The proper interpretation of the teaching about happiness), he points out that the maturity that brings man closer to God also brings him closer to himself. Commenting on the Christian call to perfection (cf. Mt 5:48), he writes: "This perfection is not heteronomous—it does not deprive man of what he is or should be. On the contrary, it addresses his very essence. Perfection always is humanistic, internal, and human."[110]

Reading *Elements of Ethics,* one wonders why Wojtyła did not give to his reflections the more adequate title *Elements of Christian Ethics* or *Elements of Moral Theology*. It seems that by using the title *Elements of Ethics,* he wanted to emphasize the more universal character of his reflections as well as the significance of the dialogue between reason and faith, philosophy and theology, for every human person, believer and unbeliever.

Wojtyła's sound statement about the Christian inspiration of his philosophy and about his intellectual debt to Etienne Gilson can be found in his 1962 introduction to the second Polish edition of *Miłość i odpowiedzialność* (Love and responsibility). Writing about the intellectual sources of his book, Wojtyła pointed to the texts of the New Testament that deal with sexual and marital morality.[111] Then, he writes:

---

109. Ibid., 138–39; cf. "Religijne rozumienie czystości," 55.
110. *Aby Chrystus,* 157.
111. Mt 5:27–28; Mt 19:1–13; Mk 10:1–12; Lk 20:27–35.

"One knows that in Revelation originated not only a theology that employed philosophy as a tool for intellectual speculation. Revelation also provided a significant inspiration for philosophy—it is enough to mention the theory of existence developed by St. Thomas. It seems that in a similar manner the Gospel provides inspiration for philosophical reflection about sexual problems."[112] He emphasizes that, despite the inspiration taken from the New Testament, *Love and Responsibility* remains a philosophical and not a theological book. However, in a manner similar to that already pointed out in *Elements of Ethics,* philosophy and theology remain in a continuous dialogue throughout the book. For example, Wojtyła's criticism of utilitarian ethics is followed by a section called "Przykazanie miłości a norma personalistyczna" (The commandment to love and the personalistic norm), where he points out that the New Testament's highest commandment stands in radical contradiction to the utilitarian norm.[113] In the next chapter, which compares different interpretations of sexual desire, Wojtyła starts with a religious interpretation based on Christian revelation.[114] Wojtyła's reflections on justice toward the Creator—especially in the sections pertaining to the human vocation—clearly have in the background, not the First Cause of Aristotle, but the God of the Judeo-Christian tradition.[115]

Central to Wojtyła's argument in *Love and Responsibility* is the personalist norm *(norma personalistyczna),* which says that no human person should be treated as a means, but rather each person should be treated only as an end of human actions.[116] This norm presupposes a personalist anthropology that describes the human person as

112. *Miłość,* 18.   113. Ibid., 36–45 (31–45).
114. Ibid., 53–56 (54–57).   115. Ibid., 219–35 (245–65).
116. Ibid., 21–45 (21–45). This formulation of the personalist norm stems from Immanuel Kant, who was influenced by Christian pietism (cf. Immanuel Kant, *Grounding for the Metaphysics of Morals,* trans. James W. Ellington [Indianapolis: Hackett Publishing Company, 1993] 36).

possessing a unique dignity as well as enjoying personal freedom and the possibility of knowing the truth. In the introduction to *Love and Responsibility*, Wojtyła emphasized that this notion of *persona* was created in Western culture in the context of Judeo-Christian revelation.[117] Having such a religious origin, the notion was generally considered to be the cornerstone of Western civilization. In recent centuries it has even become an argument against Christianity, in that Christianity supposedly deprives free human beings of their autonomy.[118] However, when the personalist anthropology is detached from its religious roots, it loses its *raison d'être*, as John Paul II emphasized in *Evangelium Vitae*, 22:

When the sense of God is lost, the sense of man is also threatened and poisoned . . . Man is no longer able to see himself as "mysteriously different" from other earthly creatures; he regards himself merely as one more living being, as an organism which, at most, has reached a very high stage of perfection. Enclosed in the narrow horizon of his physical nature, he is somehow reduced to being "a thing" and no longer grasps the "transcendent" character of his "existence as man."[119]

This argument of John Paul II shows a close affinity with that published forty years earlier in *Love and Responsibility*, which based its personalistic norm on the fundamental distinction between the human person and a thing.[120] The topic of the unique dignity of the human person who transcends all other creatures is also present in *The Acting Person*, which in all Polish editions begins with this quota-

117. *Miłość*, 19. For Christian origins of personalist anthropology see Ernst-Wolfgang Böckenförde. "Kościół a nowoczesny świat," in Böckenförde, *Wolność—państwo—Kościół* (Kraków: Znak, 1994), 211; Schmitz, *At the Center*, 39–40.

118. John Paul II. *Crossing the Threshold of Hope* (New York: Alfred A. Knopf, Inc., 1994), 50–53.

119. *Origins*, vol. 24, no. 42 (1995), 697.

120. *Miłość*, 23–26 (21–25).

tion from *Gaudium et Spes, 77*: "The role and competence of the Church being what it is, she must in no way be confused with the political community, not bound to any political system. For she is at once a sign and a safeguard of the transcendence of the human person."[121]

Wojtyła wrote *The Acting Person* during the Second Vatican Council, possibly even working on it during the official gatherings of the Council Fathers.[122] He admits in the book that the Council provided him with rich inspiration in his thinking about man.[123] In regard to its Christian character, the style of Wojtyła's philosophical thinking in *The Acting Person* shows many similarities with that in the *Lublin Lectures, Elements of Ethics,* and *Love and Responsibility:* an openness to further theological reflections; a constant dialogue with theology; the Christian assumption that the human person enjoys a unique dignity among all other creatures.

One more remark is needed to complete these reflections about the Christian character of Wojtyła's philosophy. Central to his account of the acting person is the notion of the human will. In his analysis of the will, Wojtyła is especially indebted to Thomas Aquinas and twentieth-century experimental psychology.[124] However, a compelling argument can be made that Wojtyła's notion of will, as with his notion of *persona,* was formulated within a distinctly Christian intellectual framework.

Charles Kahn writes in his illuminating article "Discovering the Will: From Aristotle to Augustine," that there has been general agreement among scholars that the notion of the will was lacking in Greek

121. *Decrees,* vol. II, 1081.
122. An anecdote says that John Paul I during a conversation with Cardinal Wojtyła said: "I remember you very well from the Council. Your seat was not far from mine and I could see you constantly writing."
123. *Osoba,* 71 (302–3).
124. Cf. above, 35–38.

philosophy.[125] In his classic book *Will in Western Thought: An Historico-Critical Survey*, Vernon Bourke also classifies Socrates, Plato, and Aristotle as ethical intellectualists. They all associated the notion of willing very closely with the act of intellectual preference. They hold, Bourke writes, that "willing is basically a cognitive function of judging that one object of consideration is to be set above others."[126]

A crucial development in the theory of the will is attributed by historians to St. Augustine. Bourke classifies Augustine among thinkers who express their views in what may be called "heart-language." Among those thinkers, the heart is understood as the center of the human person, "the seat of the highest spiritual affections, of the most intimate knowledge, and decisions."[127] In this theory, love is understood as the central or distinctive function of volition. Bourke points out two ancient sources of this ethical theory: ancient Greek medicine and the Bible.

Following the arguments of another distinguished scholar in ancient philosophy, Albrecht Dihle, Kahn seems to agree with Bourke in regard to the biblical influences on Augustine's theory of the will.

The concept of the will as a factor or aspect of the personality distinct from, and irreducible to, intellect and desire or reason and emotion is completely absent from the Greek tradition but implicit from the beginning in the biblical notion of obedience to the commands of God. To obey God is to do as he

---

125. In: I. M. Dillon and A. A. Long, *The Question of "Eclecticism": Studies in Later Greek Philosophy* (Berkeley: University of California Press, 1988), 234. Recently, A. J. Voelke (*L'idée de volonté dans le stoïcisme* [Paris, 1973]) and A. J. P. Kenny (*Aristotle's Theory of the Will* [New Haven: Yale University Press, 1979]) challenged this assumption. Kahn comments on their conclusions: "The authors of these two books would probably accept the view that the ancients did not have 'our' concept of the will: their books describe ancient theories that cover the same ground that we would think of as belonging to the topic of the will" (Kahn, 234).

126. New York: Sheed and Ward, 1964, p. 29.

127. Ibid., 13.

wishes, to comply with his will, although this will may be entirely inscrutable. ... The appropriate human response is to be seen neither in terms of rational understanding nor in terms of emotions and desire, but as a commitment of the whole person that calls out for the concept of will for its articulation.[128]

Kahn points out that the concept of will gets its full philosophical articulation in the fourth century, "first in the Trinitarian debates which provide a coherent doctrine of the divine will, and then in Augustine's theoretical reflections on his own experience of conversion and on the consequent need for clarifying his notion of the human will *(voluntas)* in the face of Manichean dualism."[129]

As Kahn suggests, Augustine's description of his conversion in the *Confessions* shows clearly some elements of his concept of the will.[130] Augustine writes about two wills that are in a conflict with each other. The old will is carnal, the new one is spiritual. The old will is in the power of an "enemy," namely passion and sin. Augustine writes, therefore, that he was held fast by the iron of his own perverse, old will that prevented him from turning away from sin to God. The new will *(voluntas nova)*, however, becomes in Augustine the source of a new, religious zeal and love for God.[131]

Kahn emphasizes that regarding the theory of human will there is a serious disadvantage in stopping with Augustine.

Augustine begins but does not complete the task of working out a Christian theory of the will. Augustine was a religious genius, but he was not a profes-

---

128. Kahn, 236–37. Cf. Albrecht Dihle, *The Theory of Will in Classical Antiquity* (Berkeley and Los Angeles: University of California Press, 1982), 123–44.

129. Kahn, 237.

130. Augustine, *Confessions* 8.5; CCL 27.119–20.

131. Augustine's analysis of his own conversion seems to be patterned after St. Paul's description of his spiritual journey. Two texts of St. Paul in particular may have inspired Augustine—St.Paul's distinction between the old and the new man (Eph 4:17–24) and his famous analysis of the inner conflict in his soul (Rom 7:14–20).

sionally trained philosopher: he had neither the inclination nor the technical equipment to formulate his conception of the will within the framework of a systematic theory of human action. Augustine's concept of the will does not get a fully philosophical development until it is integrated within the theoretical model for the psyche, namely, Aristotle's. This synthesis of Augustinian will with Aristotelian philosophy of mind is the work of Thomas Aquinas.[132]

* * *

The starting point of Wojtyła's theory of the acting person is human experience, which is objectivized in the process of induction and then explored by reduction. It would seem that the last stage of this theory should consist of a certain hermeneutics whereby an historical analysis might reveal some of the theory's hidden presuppositions, especially those coming from the Christian faith of the philosopher. This hermeneutics is needed because secularized modern culture rejects the classic theory of *persona* and the human soul, replacing it with theories of the self, the subject, the individual, etc.[133] Similar moves can be observed with regard to other anthropological concepts: freedom, conscience, ethical values, human rights, nature, etc. In the face of the modern deconstruction of anthropology, an historical hermeneutics, by tracing the origins of different anthropological concepts, may (1) identify the Christian contribution to contemporary anthropology (2) provide some arguments in a confrontation with modern and post-modern deconstruction, and (3) provide the basis for a modern Christian apologetics aware of the Christian contributions to Western culture.[134]

---

132. Kahn, 237–38. As was already pointed out, Wojtyła is greatly indebted to Aquinas's theory of the will, though he shapes it with his personalism.

133. Cf. Schmitz, *At the Center,* 39–40.

134. An excellent example of such an historical hermeneutics in the area of moral virtue is Alasdair MacIntyre, *After Virtue: A Study in Moral Theory* (Notre Dame: University of Notre Dame Press, 1981).

CHAPTER 4

Consciousness and Efficacy

THE PHENOMENON OF human efficient causality reveals itself most completely in the conscious act of the person.[1] Thus, in *The Acting Person*, Wojtyła's analysis of human causality is preceded by his theory of consciousness. Wojtyła's treatment of human consciousness clearly manifests his methodological and epistemological assumptions that result in his philosophical differences from classic phenomenology and modern idealism, as well as from twentieth-century neo-Thomism. But before giving a detailed account of Wojtyła's mature theory of human efficacy, it is necessary to present the main principles of his theory of consciousness.

CONSCIOUSNESS

Before Wojtyła outlined for the first time his theory of human consciousness in *The Acting Person*, he suggested in a number of articles that the traditional anthropology should be supplemented with a theory of consciousness. In the article "Personalizm tomistyczny" (Thomistic personalism) from 1961, Wojtyła compares modern anthropol-

---

1. Wojtyła begins the first chapter of *The Acting Person* with the discussion of the Polish word "*czyn*," which is used in the title of the book. *Czyn* in Polish means a conscious action of the human agent. Therefore, it can be translated into Latin as *actus humanus* or even *actus voluntarius* (cf. *Osoba*, 73–74 [25–26]).

ogy with the Thomistic concept of person. After Descartes, he writes, anthropology concentrated mostly on the analysis of consciousness, which was almost completely identified with the whole person. This led to a dualistic treatment of the person: "Consciousness is an object of internal experience, which consists in introspection, while the body, like everything else in nature, is an object of observation and external experience. This concept fails to incorporate the body into the life and activity of the whole person."[2] Wojtyła emphasized that Thomas Aquinas presented a totally different picture of the person, where consciousness is only an accident of the rational nature of the human. Aquinas did not concentrate on the analysis of consciousness. However, consciousness is implicitly present in the Thomistic concept of *actus humanus,* especially in its analysis of human rational nature, and in its concept of the rationality of the will.[3] Wojtyła emphasized that the task of a contemporary Christian philosopher is to supplement the traditional concept of *persona humana* with a theory of consciousness.[4]

Beginning his treatment of consciousness in *The Acting Person* with a thesis that clearly separates him from most of the thinkers of the phenomenological tradition, he states that the fundamental function of consciousness consists not in intentional cognition but in mirroring the objects that are already known to the subject. Consciousness is "an understanding of what has already been understood."[5] His rejection of the intentional character of consciousness has to be prop-

---

2. *Aby Chrystus,* 435. John Paul II identified Descartes as the founder of the modern dualistic anthropology (cf. *Crossing the Threshold,* 50–52). Also, according to the Pope, the dualism in anthropology is the cause of many contemporary ethical problems (cf. *"Letter to Families,"* 19).

3. Cf. *Osoba,* 78–79 (30–31).

4. Cf. "Etyka a teologia moralna" (Ethics and moral theology), in *Aby Chrystus,* 465.

5. *Osoba,* 81 (32).

erly understood. Husserl defined intentionality as "the unique peculiarity of experiences to be always the consciousness of something."[6]
Wojtyła does not deny that consciousness always is a consciousness of
something. Rather, since he based his anthropological reflections on
the Aristotelian notion of act, he also defined the intentionality of
human cognition in a way different from Husserl. For Wojtyła, intention consists in an active directing upon the object. Therefore, only the
real cognitive faculties of the person, knowledge and self-knowledge,
possess such intentional character. Consciousness only mirrors the
outcome of the cognitive process of knowledge and self-knowledge.

Wojtyła defined self-knowledge as the understanding of one's own
self and a cognitive insight into the object that I am for myself. Since
self-knowledge is concerned with the ego, its cognitive process must
also be relevant for consciousness. Wojtyła reflects on the relation
between self-knowledge and consciousness:

Consciousness, for all the intimacy of its subjective union with the ego, does
not objectivize the ego or anything else with regard to its existence and its acting. This function is performed by acts of self-knowledge themselves. It is to
them that every man owes the objectivizing contact with himself and with his
actions. Because of self-knowledge, consciousness can mirror actions and
their relations to the ego. Without it, consciousness would be deprived of its
immanent meanings so far as man's self is concerned . . .[7]

According to Wojtyła, self-knowledge grasps the acting subject's ego as
an object. Consciousness itself is also an object of self-knowledge
when the subject knows that he acts and that he acts consciously. Because of the objectivization of consciousness through self-knowledge,
Wojtyła insists, consciousness is rooted in the existence of the subject.

6. Ibid., 80 (303–4).
7. Ibid., 85 (36).

Therefore, the acceptance of self-knowledge's objectivizing function is a necessary condition for a realistic theory of consciousness. Otherwise, a philosopher ends up with some kind of idealism.

Also according to Wojtyła, besides mirroring, consciousness brings into prominence in human experience the subjectiveness of the subject. This other function of consciousness Wojtyła calls "reflexive."[8] Traditional ontology used the Latin word *suppositum* to denote man as the subject of his being and acting, Wojtyła continues. The term *suppositum* does not describe, however, the reflexive aspect of consciousness, owing to which the concrete man experiences himself as the distinct subject. For this reason, the term "I" is more comprehensive than the notion *suppositum* since it combines the moment of experienced subjectiveness with that of ontic subjectiveness.[9]

Due to the reflexive function of consciousness, the human subject experiences his own actions and their moral values in relation to his own ego.

Objectively, both action and moral values belong to a real subject, that is, to man as their agent . . . Simultaneously, both the action and its corresponding moral value—goodness or badness—function, if we may say so, in a thoroughly subjective manner in experience—which consciousness conditions by its reflexive function rather than only mirroring it because of self-knowledge, for this would still give but an objectified awareness of the action and its moral value.[10]

---

8. The beginnings of Wojtyła's theory of the two functions of consciousness, mirroring and reflexive, can be traced to *Love and Responsibility* where, in Wojtyła's psychological analysis of love, he states: "Human cognition does not consist merely in reflecting or producing 'mirror image' of objects, but is inseparable from awareness of truth and falsehood" (*Miłość*, 103 [115]). In *Love and Responsibility*, though, Wojtyła did not yet make a clear distinction between human intentional cognition and consciousness.

9. *Osoba*, 92–93 (44–45).

10. Ibid., 97 (48–49).

Wojtyła emphasizes the importance of the subject's reflexive experience both of his own actions and of moral values. Through the reflexive function of consciousness, they become the subjective reality of the person who experiences himself as the cause of his own actions and, therefore, as the one who is either morally good or morally evil.

Also, the subject's body is present in the mirroring and reflexive dimension of consciousness. Wojtyła indicates that the self-knowledge of the body—which is prior to the body's presence in consciousness—starts with particular bodily sensations.

Self-knowledge, and with it consciousness, reaches only as far, or rather as deep, into the organism and its life as sensations allow it to reach. Very often, for instance, owing to disease, which activates the corresponding bodily sensations, man becomes aware of one of his organs or of a vegetative process within himself. Generally, the human body and everything associated with it become the object of sensations first, and only subsequently of self-knowledge and consciousness.[11]

In a clear reference to Descartes's rationalistic and dualistic anthropology, Wojtyła emphasizes that man is not only a thinking but also a feeling creature. The world of human feelings and sensations has an amazing wealth which is characterized by a certain hierarchical order. One can distinguish lower and higher sensations; some of them participate even in the spiritual life of the person. Wojtyła points out that all those emotions are not only reflected in the mirroring dimension of consciousness. They also affect the image that is formed in consciousness of various objects, including man's ego and his actions. "Diverse feelings emotionalize consciousness, that is to say, they blend with its two functions—mirroring and reflexiveness—thereby modifying in one way or another their character. This is first manifested in

11. Ibid., 100 (51).

the image formed in consciousness, which, so to speak, loses its aloofness with regard to emotion and the objects to which emotion is attached."[12] Normally, an aloofness of consciousness is a result of the self-knowledge which is able to objectivize human emotions. Through this objectivization, the meaning of the emotive facts is accessible to consciousness, which is then able to control them.[13] Wojtyła emphasizes that this control over the emotions is of great importance for the inner integration of the human person. The process in which consciousness loses its control over emotions is called by Wojtyła "the emotionalization of consciousness."

The emotionalization of consciousness begins when the image of the meanings of the particular emotive instances and of objects they are related to fades in consciousness, so that feelings may outgrow their current understanding by man. This is practically tantamount to a breakdown of self-knowledge; for consciousness, without ceasing to mirror the emotive instances just as they come, loses its controlling, that is to say, its objective attitude toward them.[14]

Wojtyła mentions two possible reasons for the emotionalization of consciousness. The first one points to the intensity and changeability of emotions, which makes them difficult to control. The other one, more significant, consists in the weakness of self-knowledge, which is not able to objectivize the emotions efficiently. Then, consciousness does not mirror feelings as "something that happens in me" but rather

12. Ibid., 102 (52–53).
13. The phrase "consciousness's control over the emotions" has to be understood analogically. Strictly speaking, it is not consciousness that controls emotions, since consciousness does not have an intentional character, and since a participation of the will is required for this control. However, the person's control over emotions is visible through consciousness, when self-knowledge creates a certain aloofness of consciousness in regard to the emotions, and the reflexive function of consciousness is able to link the emotive facts to the "I" of the subject.
14. *Osoba*, 102 (53).

as "something that happens"—the emotions' link with the ego is broken.

Wojtyła points out that the emotionalization of consciousness touches not only the mirroring but also the reflexive function of consciousness. In the most intense stage of emotionalization, consciousness still mirrors the emotions, but the reflexive function of consciousness disappears.

It is remarkable that emotions and passions are not experienced by the human being when too strong; they are then only "undergone" by him or, strictly speaking, allowed to grow in him and prevail upon him in some primitive and, as it were, impersonal fashion; for "personal" signifies only that experience in which also the experienced subjectiveness of the ego is to be discerned.[15]

Wojtyła's theory of consciousness is thoroughly realistic. He rejected the intentionality of consciousness in order to insist on the direct dependence of consciousness on other cognitive faculties of the human person. In this way, he successfully avoided this danger of modern idealism: that it tends to treat consciousness almost as an independent subject, separated from the rest of the human person, especially the human body. Also, Wojtyła's emphasis on the mirroring function of consciousness points to an existence of the real world outside of consciousness.[16]

EFFICACY

Wojtyła applies his theory of consciousness, the one outlined above, to describe human causal efficacy. He starts with an observation that only a part of human activity is mirrored by consciousness.

---

15. Ibid., 104 (55).
16. Schmitz finds similarities between Wojtyła's theory of the mirroring consciousness and the medieval description of the human theoretical activity that employed Latin terms like *speculum, speculari,* and *speculatio* (cf. Schmitz, *At the Center,* 71–72).

For example, the human person is unaware of most of his own vegetative processes. Also, subconsciousness is *per definitionem* absent
from the consciousness.[17] The reflection on the relation of different
kinds of human activity to consciousness led Wojtyła to distinguish
two fundamental kinds of human activity: (1) man acts, and (2)
something is happening in man. He writes that the former reveals
the fully human, conscious activity of the subject *(agere)* while the
latter, which he also calls an activation of the human dynamism
(uczynnienie), points to his passivity *(pati)*.[18] The essential difference between *agere* and *pati* consists in the subject's experience of
being the cause of a specific deed. "When acting I have the experience of myself as the agent responsible for this particular form of
dynamization of myself as the subject. When there is something
happening in me, then the dynamism is imparted without the efficacious participation of my ego."[19]

Wojtyła writes that these two fundamental kinds of human activity, happening and acting, reveal two different aspects of the human
person. Happening seems to reveal human subjectiveness while acting
points to human efficacy. "Man has the experience of himself as the
subject when something is happening in him; when, on the other side,

17. The analysis of Wojtyła's treatment of human vegetative processes will be presented in the next chapter, in the section devoted to Wojtyła's account of human integration. Wojtyła's analysis of human subconsciousness is presented at the end of this
section.

18. Wojtyła's description of *agere* corresponds to Thomas Aquinas's definition of
actus humanus as distinguished from *actus hominis* (cf. *ST* Ia IIae, q.1, a.1). With his theory of human consciousness, however, Wojtyła seems to be able to penetrate more than
Aquinas into the structure of *actus humanus*. The distinction between *agere* and *pati*
was defined by Wojtyła for the first time in the late 1950s, in his publications devoted to
the analysis of human love. It seems that the difference between an emotion of love and
a fully human, mature act of love became a starting point for his reflections on the difference between *pati* and *agere* (cf. above, chapter 2, note 92).

19. *Osoba*, 116 (66).

he is acting, he has the experience of himself as the 'actor'..."[20] Human subjectiveness and efficacy then seem to divide the field of human experiences into two mutually irreducible areas. On the other hand, there is a profound unity between *pati* and *agere,* since they are both rooted in the human person. In order to resolve this paradox, Wojtyła distinguishes two different meanings of human subjectivity: (1) subjectivity as revealed by what is happening in man, and (2) subject as the common root of both acting and happening.

Wojtyła points out that the latter understanding of the human subject was expressed·in Aristotelian-Thomistic philosophy by the Latin word *suppositum.* Etymologically, *suppositum* indicates what is placed under *(sub-ponere).* In anthropology, Wojtyła writes, it is the subject who is "under" every acting and happening. The subject is here understood as a real being, which according to the classic adage "*operari sequitur esse*" makes possible every kind of human dynamism, both *agere* and *pati.*[21]

While introducing some notions of Aristotelian-Thomistic ontology to his anthropology, Wojtyła points to their limitations. For example, defining the human subject as *suppositum,* he emphasizes the essential difference that exists between human *suppositum* and any other inanimate *suppositum* which is the difference between somebody and something. He also expresses some reservation toward Boethius's definition of the human person: "*persona est individua substantia rationalis naturae*" (the person is an individual substance of rational nature). According to Wojtyła, neither *individua substantia* nor *natura rationalis* adequately defines the human person.[22]

In the article "Subjectivity and the Irreducible in Man," written seven years after the publication of the first edition of *Osoba i czyn,*

---

20. Ibid., 121 (71).   21. Ibid., 122 (72–73).
22. Cf. ibid., 123 (73–74).

Wojtyła distinguished two different ways of defining man, cosmological and personalistic.[23] The examples of the former definition are: (1) Aristotle's formula "*homo est animal rationale,*" and (2) Boetius's definition "*rationalis naturae individua substantia.*" At the core of every cosmological definition of man, Wojtyła indicates, there is an assumption that the essence of man can be described by a comparison with the rest of the world. The human phenomenon appears as an object homogenous with other objects in the universe and reducible to them. Wojtyła points out that the cosmological definition can be helpful in explaining the human phenomenon, but it is not able to reveal what is specific, unique, and irreducible in the human person. There is an element that is missing from the cosmological definition, Wojtyła indicates, and that element consists in the human experience that is able to reveal the uniquely human personal subjectiveness. The theory which defines the human person through what is irreducible is called by Wojtyła "personalistic."

"Nature" is the next notion from the Aristotelian-Thomistic anthropology that Wojtyła analyzes in order to incorporate it, eventually, into his own philosophy of the acting person. "Etymologically the term 'nature' is . . . derived from the Latin verb *nascor* ('to be born'), hence natus ('born') and *naturus* ('about to be born'). Thus 'nature' denotes literally everything that is going to be born or is contained in the fact itself of birth as its possible consequence."[24]

Wojtyła indicates that the word "nature" has many different meanings. It can denote the material world, both animate and inanimate; in the latter case, however, it goes beyond its etymological roots. Also, one speaks about human, animal, or vegetative nature, where "nature"

---

23. *Analecta Husserliana* 7 (1978), 107–14.
24. *Osoba*, 125 (76).

refers to some property of a specific subject that can be also expressed by the word "essence." Wojtyła points out that "nature" does not denote any real and actual subject of existence and, therefore, it can not be identified with *suppositum*. Primarily, *natura humana* refers to an abstract being which stands in relation to all men by pointing out the specific traits common to all human beings by the very fact of their being human.

Wojtyła insists that the word "nature," in accord with its etymological roots, refers not only to the subject of human activity but also seems to point out a specific manner of human dynamization. "Nature ... tells of what is about to be born and what is contained in the fact of birth itself as its possible consequence. The fact of birth is in itself something dynamic; but it also marks the beginning of the dynamism proper to the subject that is being born."[25] Building his phenomenological description on the etymological analysis of the word "nature," Wojtyła states that the moment of happening in the subject *(pati)* most fully reveals human nature. He explains:

The concept of nature includes that dynamism which is directly and solely the consequence of birth itself; the dynamism that is inclusively inborn or innate, exclusively immanent in the given subject of acting, as if it was determined in advance by its properties. Nature reveals the dynamism of the subject, that is, it reveals that activeness which is wholly and entirely contained in the subject's dynamic readiness; as if this activeness was from the start an attribute of the subject and was entirely prepared in its subjective dynamic structure.[26]

Wojtyła points out that nature is understood here not as the source of every human dynamism, which would be closer to the Aristotelian-

25. Ibid., 126 (77–78).
26. Ibid., 127 (78).

Thomistic definition of *natura humana*. The phenomenological description of nature, he insists, points to what is happening in the subject *(pati)* while the human conscious actions *(agere)* seem to refer to the conscious "I," that is the person, as their cause. This is why in the phenomenological analysis there is a difference and even an opposition between nature and the person.

This line of reasoning, Wojtyła emphasizes, cannot stop here. So far, the etymological and phenomenological analysis has described nature only insofar as it refers to a certain manner of human dynamism. What is necessary for a completion of this analysis, though, is a fuller description of the subject of both acting and happening. This description requires the creation of a synthesis of happening and acting, subjectivity and efficacy, nature and person, since all these notions describe only one aspect of the human phenomenon and ultimately all are rooted in the same *suppositum*. Wojtyła begins to create this synthesis with the thesis that all kinds of human experience culminate and are summoned in the experience of one's own ego.

It is the ego that is the agent of actions. When man acts, the ego has the experience of its own efficacy in action. When, on the other hand, there is something happening in man, then the ego does not experience its own efficacy and is not the actor, but it does have the experience of the inner identity of itself with what is happening and, at the same time, of the exclusive dependence of what is happening to itself.[27]

Wojtyła emphasizes that any rejection of the dependency both of happening and acting on the ego contradicts a fundamental human experience. Also, he insists that the emphasis on the dependence of both happening and acting on the ego neutralizes the opposition between nature and the person. *Natura* and *persona* still remain the

27. *Osoba*, 129 (80).

causes of different kinds of human dynamism, but they are both rooted in the ego.[28]

The phenomenological description of human nature should be supplemented by metaphysical analysis, he insists. Metaphysically, "nature" is a synonym for "essence" and means here humanness as the source of every human dynamism. Wojtyła points out that the relation between human nature and human activity is well summarized by the old adage "*operari sequitur esse.*" First, this statement points out that in order to act, one has to exist. Second, there is a cohesion between any kind of human activity and its source, which is the person. Wojtyła insists that this cohesion can be expressed only by the concept of nature. "Nature provides the basis for the essential cohesion of the subject of dynamism with all the dynamism of the subject. The attributive *all* is important, because it allows us to reject once and for all the meaning of nature which exhibits it as only a moment and only one mode of the dynamization of the subject."[29]

Wojtyła makes clear that the metaphysical description of nature corresponds to all kinds of human activity and not only to *pati* as is the case in the phenomenological analysis. Also, he emphasizes that the human experience of the cohesion between *operari* and *esse* leads to an understanding of how the nature is integrated in the person. This integration does not consist in the individualization of nature by the person, as a strict reading of Boethius's definition of *persona humana* would suggest.

---

28. Wojtyła writes: "Integration does not abolish the differences in the manner *suppositum* is dynamized, but simply prevents any tendency to treat person and nature as two separate and independent subjects of being" (ibid., 129 [81]). One may notice how Wojtyła's analysis is constantly underlined by his polemics with anthropological dualism, which *de facto* divides man into two different things: consciousness and body, or person and nature.

29. Ibid., 131.

The person is not merely an "individualized humanness": it actually consists rather in the mode of individual being that pertains (from among all the types of existing beings) to mankind alone. This mode of being stems from the fact that the peculiar type of being proper to mankind is personal.[30]

In his analysis of the notions "subject" and "nature," Wojtyła follows the method defined in his first of the *Lublin Lectures*, "Ethical Act and Ethical Experience."[31] This method consists of the two steps, phenomenological description and metaphysical synthesis. The phenomenology is useful as the starting point, Wojtyła holds, because of its ability to discover and describe many aspects of the human phenomenon which otherwise would be unknown to a metaphysician. As we have seen earlier, however, according to Wojtyła's analysis, any phenomenological anthropology is in need of a synthesis, or integration, since it divides the human person into many irreducible aspects, as was the case with the notions of *agere* and *pati*, efficacy and subjectivity, person and nature.[32] This integration can be obtained only through a metaphysical analysis, which is able to describe the ultimate roots of all the phenomenological aspects of the human phenomenon. For Wojtyła, this ultimate foundation consists in the personal *suppositum*, which exists in a manner distinct from any other *suppositum*. This personal being is the source of all human dynamism, both *pati* and *agere*, and it reveals the rich potentiality of human nature, a dynamism only partially mirrored in consciousness.

Wojtyła concludes his reflections on the relation between consciousness and human efficacy with some thoughts about subconsciousness

30. Ibid.
31. Cf. above, 60–62.
32. There are many tendencies in modern phenomenology. For example, Husserl attempted to unite different aspects of the human phenomenon in the transcendental ego. It seems, though, that in his criticism of phenomenology, Wojtyła argues primarily with Scheler.

and human becoming. First, he elaborates the distinction between human dynamism and human potentiality. These two phenomena are inseparably linked to each other.[33] In the human experience, one encounters first the phenomenon of dynamism, which denotes every kind of dynamization of the subject, both *pati* and *agere*. This dynamism starts inside the subject and is the potentiality that defines its inner source. Ultimately, this source consists in the human *suppositum;* different potentialities, however, define more specifically different causes of human dynamism.[34]

Wojtyła distinguishes two fundamental human potentialities, the psycho-emotive and the somato-vegetative. He emphasizes that the former is clearly mirrored by consciousness, while the latter happens in man largely outside the field of consciousness. The unity and identity of the human subject, therefore, is not realized purely through consciousness; it is prior to consciousness and more fundamental. He writes: "The dynamic unity of the human subject consists primarily in the unity of life and only secondarily . . . in the unity of experience."[35] This conclusion supports the main methodological assumption of Wojtyła's adequate anthropology, which says that the human potentiality is much richer than the part of it mirrored in consciousness. Therefore, every anthropology which is limited exclusively to an analysis of consciousness does not describe the whole person.

33. Etymologically, the meaning of these two words is very similar. The Greek word "*dynamis*" means "force" or "power"; Latin word "*potentia*" refers to "power" or "faculty."

34. In his theory of human potentiality and dynamism, Wojtyła is clearly indebted to Aristotelian-Thomistic anthropology. The reasoning presented above, which leads to a definition of human faculties (*potentiae*) and then to their systematization, can be found both in Aristotle (cf. *De anima* 3.9.432–33) and in Thomas Aquinas (cf. *ST* Ia, qq. 77–83). Wojtyła's intellectual debt, however, is limited here to the definition of human potentiality, since he does not employ in his analyses the Aristotelian-Thomistic systematization of the faculties.

35. *Osoba*, 139 (91).

According to Wojtyła, the existence of human subconsciousness also proves the priority of human potentiality in regard to consciousness. In *The Acting Person,* subconsciousness is defined as "an inner space to which some objects are expelled or withheld and prevented from reaching the threshold of consciousness."[36] Subconsciousness should be clearly distinguished from simple nonconsciousness, since in subconsciousness it is the human will which is responsible for preventing some objects from crossing the threshold of consciousness. Those objects, however, remain in the subject in a dynamic condition, waiting to enter the field of consciousness, Wojtyła writes. Psychoanalytic research reveals that these objects wait for a suitable opportunity to emerge—for instance, when consciousness is weakened or inhibited by overwork or in sleep.

Wojtyła summarizes in four points the importance of the study of subconsciousness for an adequate anthropology. First, the existence of subconsciousness reveals the richness of the human potentiality, which is only partially mirrored in consciousness. Second, the study of subconsciousness can illustrate, in the continual transitions between nonconscious, subconscious, and conscious, the inner cohesion of the human subject. Third, the analysis of subconsciousness points out the importance of the historical dimension of the human person. Finally, it reveals a hierarchy that exists in human potentiality, because of the constant drive of subconsciousness toward consciousness. This pressure to cross over the threshold of consciousness points to consciousness as the sphere where man most appropriately fulfills himself.[37]

36. Ibid., 141 (93).
37. Wanda Półtawska points out the two original and inspiring elements of Wojtyła's theory of subconsciousness: (1) a nondeterministic character of subconsciousness, which is presented as an expression of human potentiality, and (2) the immanent drive of subconsciousness toward consciousness (cf. "Koncepcja samoposiadania—podstawą

Wojtyła ends his reflections on the relation between consciousness and efficacy with some remarks about the subject's becoming, *fieri*.

By "becoming" we mean such an aspect of the human dynamism—whether it is the aspect of man's acting or the aspect of what happens in him—that does not only center on man himself, the subject of this dynamism, insofar as it introduces or carries on a process of change. In point of fact, in all dynamizations the subject does not remain indifferent: not only does it participate in them . . . but it is itself in one way or another formed or transformed by them.[38]

Wojtyła points out that in every dynamization of the subject, both *pati* and *agere*, something new comes to existence in man. The conscious actions of the subject *(agere)* have a special importance for the person's becoming, since through them the subject becomes morally good or morally bad. Wojtyła presents morality not as an abstract idea but as an existential reality of the person who creates himself.[39] Morality, therefore, is not purely an aspect of consciousness, but it describes the "becoming" of the whole human being.

---

psychoterapii obiektywizującej. W świetle książki Kardynała Karola Wojtyły *Osoba i czyn,*" *Analecta Cracoviensia* 5–6 [1973–74], 232–34).

38. *Osoba,* 144 (96).

39. Through conscious actions, the subject forms his own moral value by becoming morally good or morally evil. Therefore, Wojtyła emphasizes that, besides producing an outward effect, e.g., a sheet of paper covered with writing, the acting person first and foremost creates himself. The person is the creator while being also the raw material. Wojtyła's thoughts about human creativity presented in *The Acting Person* seem to elaborate further the main topic of his first *Lublin Lecture,* "Ethical Act and Ethical Experience," where he struggled to provide a philosophical account of how the person becomes morally good or morally evil by acting. Another source for these reflections can be found in Wojtyła's autobiographical poem "Quarry," written in 1956, which describes the effects that the hard work of quarrymen has on their psyche and spirit. It seems that the reflections found in Wojtyła's poems, the *Lublin Lectures,* and *The Acting Person* on how the human person creates himself through work, prepared the ground for John Paul II's first social encyclical *Laborem Exercens,* which presents in detail the relation between the person and his work.

* * *

In the *Lublin Lectures*, the main philosophical categories employed by Wojtyła in his explanation of the human causal efficacy consisted of the Aristotelian-Thomistic theory of potency and act and the Thomistic notion of rational will. In *The Acting Person*, Wojtyła further develops and deepens the insight of the *Lublin Lectures* by reflecting on different forms of human dynamism—psycho-emotive, somato-vegetative, conscious, subconscious—and their relation to the main anthropological principle of causal efficacy, the will.

The originality of *The Acting Person* is rooted in its mature theory of consciousness. In contrast with most of the phenomenological tradition, Wojtyła rejects the intentionality of consciousness. Wojtyła also emphasizes the limits of consciousness by describing the human dynamism that is not mirrored by consciousness, e.g., the somato-vegetative processes and subconsciousness.

His methodology is a most interesting part of Wojtyła's analyses of the relation between human consciousness and the subject's causal efficacy. He starts with a phenomenological description of different aspects of an analyzed phenomenon in order to integrate later all these aspects by using metaphysical notions like *suppositum* or being. In the next chapter we will look at more examples of Wojtyła's phenomenological-metaphysical synthesis.

CHAPTER 5

Transcendence and Integration

E TYMOLOGICALLY, TRANSCENDENCE MEANS to go beyond a threshold or boundary *(transcendere)*. Wojtyła points
out that in the domain of human action, transcendence has
two different dimensions, horizontal and vertical. The former refers
to a situation in which, in the intentional acts of cognition and volition, the subject steps out of his limits toward an object. The latter
kind of transcendence points to the person's self-determination and
freedom.[1]

SELF-DETERMINATION

Wojtyła begins his theory of self-determination with some reflections about human freedom.[2] The subject's freedom is most visible in
human actions *(agere)* by which the person becomes morally good or
morally evil. The specific experience that points to human freedom
can be described as "I may but I do not have to." Also, the existence of
human freedom, Wojtyła continues, points to a potentiality of the
subject *(potentia)* which the philosophical tradition calls "the will."

1. *Osoba*, 164–65 (119).
2. A good summary of Wojtyła's theory of self-determination can be found in his article "The Structure of Self-Determination as the Core of the Theory of the Person," in
*Tommaso D'Aquino nel suo Settimo Centenario: Atti del Congresso Internazionale (Roma-
Napoli—17/24 Aprile 1974)* (Napoli: Edizioni Domenicane Italiane, 1978), vol. 7, 37–45.

Self-determination he then defines as the relation between the agent and his will. "Every action confirms and at the same time makes more concrete the relation, in which the will manifests itself as a feature of the person and the person manifests himself as a reality with regard to his dynamism that is properly constituted by the will. It is this relation that we call "'self-determination.'"[3]

Wojtyła indicates that personal self-determination has to be seen in the light of the process of the subject's becoming *(fieri)*.[4] Also, he continues, self-determination points to the two other aspects of the human action, self-possession and self-governance. "Because 'I will' is an act of self-determination at a particular moment, it presupposes structural self-possession. For only the things that are man's actual possession can be determined by him; they can be determined only by the one who actually possesses them. Being in the possession of himself, man can determine himself."[5]

Ever since he wrote *The Acting Person*, the concept of self-possession has been an important part of Wojtyła's anthropology. In his 1974 article "Rodzina jako *communio personarum*" (The family as *communio personarum*), while commenting on the thesis of *Gaudium et Spes* that "man . . . can attain his full identity only in sincere self-giving," Wojtyła emphasizes that the ability to become a gift for others is rooted in the subject's self-possession.[6] Also, the concept of self-

---

3. *Osoba*, 151 (105). In *The Acting Person*, Wojtyła's theory of the human will draws heavily upon his conclusions from the first *Lublin Lecture*, "Ethical Act and Ethical Experience," where he acknowledged three significant contributions to his theory: Thomas Aquinas's theory of rational will, Max Scheler's ethics of values, and twentieth-century experimental psychology of will.

4. Cf. above, 111.

5. *Osoba*, 152 (106).

6. *Ateneum Kapłańskie* 66, no. 3 (1974), 351. See also Wojtyła's "The Structure of Self-determination," 43–44.

possession and self-governance was integrated by Wojtyła into his theology. In the 1975 article "Rozważania pastoralne o rodzinie" (Pastoral reflections about the family), Wojtyła writes that self-governance is the way in which Christian couples participate in the kingly dignity *(munus regale)* of Jesus Christ.[7]

Both self-possession and self-governance reveal a certain complexity of the subject. The person possesses himself but is also that which is possessed. Similarly, the person governs himself while also being that which is actually governed. Therefore, both self-possession and self-governance reveal two fundamental dimensions of the person, his subjectiveness and his objectiveness.

The objectiveness we are now considering is realized by and also manifested in self-determination. In this sense we may speak of an "objectification" that is introduced together with self-determination into the specific dynamism of the person. This objectification means that in every actual act of self-determination—in every "I will"—the self is the object, indeed the primary and nearest object.[8]

Wojtyła insists that the objectification of the subject is unique because it does not possess an intentional character. He writes that every act of the human will is intentional since when the person wants, he wants something. This turn to something, an object, indicates the

7. *Roczniki Nauk Społecznych* 3 (1975), 66. One year later, Cardinal Wojtyła repeated this thesis in a reference to all Christians in the Lenten retreat given in the Vatican to Pope Paul VI and the employees of the Holy See (cf. *Sign of Contradiction*, 141).

8. *Osoba*, 154 (108–9). In his theory of consciousness, Wojtyła already touched on the topic of the subject's objectiveness and subjectiveness in the aspect of human cognition. He insisted that the reflexive function of consciousness is responsible for the person's experience of his own subjectiveness, while self-knowledge leads to the person's objectification. Here, Wojtyła supplements the theory presented in the previous chapter by reflecting on the person's subjectiveness and objectiveness in the aspect of human volition.

will's intentional character. It is possible also for the person, Wojtyła writes, to present one's ego as an object and to turn to it with an act of intentional willing. However, this is not characteristic of self-determination. "For in self-determination we do not turn to the ego as the object, we only impart actuality to the, so to speak, ready-made objectiveness of the ego which is contained in the intra-personal relation of self-governance and self-possession."[9]

It seems that in rejecting the intentional character of self-determination, Wojtyła is returning to his polemics with Max Scheler.[10] The German phenomenologist held that the person cannot desire his own moral good because it would lead to what he called "moral Pharisaism." Instead, the human subject should turn to material values that form the proper object of human willing. In his habilitation thesis, Wojtyła repudiated Scheler's theory of "moral Pharisaism," and blamed it on Scheler's emotionalist assumptions and the natural limits of his phenomenological method. Wojtyła himself, taking the position of ontological perfectionism, emphasized that every being tends to its own perfection and that the perfection of the human person consists in moral goodness. Therefore, it is acceptable for the human subject to desire his own moral goodness.

By rejecting in *The Acting Person* the intentionality of self-determination, Wojtyła seems to emphasize a certain lack of distance existing between the objectivity and the subjectivity of the human agent, to be contrasted with the distance created by the human will directed intentionally to its other objects. In other words, Wojtyła indicates that Scheler was right in pointing out that

9. *Osoba*, 155 (109).
10. Cf. above, 11. Also, see: *The Acting Person*, 311–12 n.54.

in the human action it is not the moral goodness of the human agent that is the primary object of will. By rejecting the intentionality of self-determination, Wojtyła seems partially to justify Scheler's criticism of "moral Pharisaism" which he previously rejected in his 1953 habilitation paper.

Wojtyła's rejection of the intentionality of self-determination, though, raises some questions. It seems that in some situations, the person himself becomes the immediate object of his own will, e.g., in the case of an overweight man who every day, out of concern for his health, carefully monitors his diet. The will of this person is intentionally directed to the value of his own health and well-being. However, even in a case like that, the person's will is intentionally directed to what Scheler calls a material value, i.e., his own health. In Wojtyła's theory, self-determination seems to describe the person's becoming *(fieri)* on a much deeper, ontological level which, as Wojtyła pointed out in his habilitation thesis, was missing from Scheler's phenomenological ethics.[11]

In *The Acting Person,* Wojtyła proceeds in his analysis of human volition by pointing out its two essential elements: (1) intentionality which consists in the will's directing itself upon its objects, and (2) a nonintentional self-determination which objectivizes the human subject. The presence of these two elements is necessary in order that an act of human volition may be called an act *(agere)* of will. When both self-determination and intentionality are present in an act of the will, such an act reveals most completely human causal efficacy and human transcendence. "At any rate, [transcendence] is connected with self-determination and the objectification peculiar to self-determination and not solely with the human ego's 'subjectiveness'

11. Cf. chapter 2.

or the intentionality of volitions that arise within the ego and are directed outward to various values as their goal."[12]

Wojtyła writes that in the process of self-determination, the will is governed by an objectifying cognition as expressed in the classic adage "*nihil volitum nisi precognitum*" (nothing is desired unless it is earlier known). This cognition cannot be provided by consciousness, since consciousness leads to the subject's experience of his own subjectiveness.[13] Therefore, Wojtyła concludes, it is the person's knowledge and self-knowledge which guide the will.

Wojtyła's treatment of human practical cognition deserves attention and careful examination. He holds that practical cognition is performed primarily by human conscience, which informs the agent about the objective truth of different goods and indicates the moral value of particular actions.[14] There are some interesting analogies between Wojtyła's treatment of theoretical cognition and his treatment of practical cognition. In regard to the former, he rejected intentionality of consciousness because of his attachment to the Aristotelian-Thomistic epistemology.[15] In regard to the latter, one can also perceive the influence of Aquinas's metaphysical anthropology on Wojtyła's theory of conscience.[16]

Wojtyła's introduction to the theory of transcendence reveals also his criticism both of phenomenology and of Aristotelian-Thomistic anthropology. On the one hand, he continues to point out the limitations of the role of consciousness in human action. According to Wojtyła, it is not the subjectivizing consciousness that guides the human will but the objectifying knowledge and self-knowledge. On

12. *Osoba*, 157 (111).
13. Cf. above, 98.
14. Wojtyła's theory of conscience is presented in chapter 4.
15. Cf. above, 96–97.
16. Cf. below, 128.

the other hand, he emphasizes that the Aristotelian-Thomistic analysis of human volition is somehow one-sided; i.e., it is too focused on the intentional willing directed to an outside object. Concentrated on horizontal transcendence, this ontological anthropology describes well *persona in actu* but not *actus personae*. In the philosophical analysis of human volition, Wojtyła finds another proof legitimizing his main methodological principle according to which the Aristotelian-Thomistic theory of human action has to be supplemented by phenomenological analysis.

He proceeds to elaborate his theory of human freedom. First, he spells out his fundamental methodological assumption: freedom has to be analyzed as an aspect of the human person and of the human will. This assumption is of great significance, Wojtyła continues, since modern philosophy has often treated the topic of freedom idealistically, as a reality detached from the real human person. The best example of such a mistake can be found in Immanuel Kant's theory of "pure freedom" and "pure morality."[17]

Wojtyła indicates that the idealistic position identifies freedom with independence and autonomy.[18] Then, he goes to the heart of his original and interesting theory of freedom by stating that the contrary is true; the essence of human freedom consists in the dependence on the subject's ego. "The lack of dependence on one's own ego in a dynamization of the subject can be identified with a lack of freedom or a lack of a basis of freedom."[19] He emphasizes that the experience of the person's dependence on one's own ego draws the line between the world of persons and the world of animals. In the former, the reflexive

17. *Osoba*, 161 (115–16).
18. As early as 1958, Wojtyła criticized in his article "Boże Narodzenie 1958" (Christmas 1958) the idealistic notion of freedom, writing that "an unlimited independence is . . . a contradiction of human freedom" (*Aby Chrystus*, 72–73).
19. *Osoba*, 163 (118).

function of consciousness leads to an experience of one's own subjectiveness and one's own ego; in the latter, all dynamizations happen on the level of nature as *pati (uczynnienia)*.[20] Also, as Wojtyła already pointed out, one of the elements of self-determination consists in a non-intentional objectification of the subject. This kind of objectification is also characteristic of free human beings; it does not happen in animals.[21]

As has already been pointed out, Wojtyła distinguished two essential elements of an act *(agere)* of will: (1) the nonintentional self-determination, which objectivizes the subject, and (2) intentionality, which consists in the will's directing itself upon its objects.[22] Similarly, he defines two meanings of human freedom. Its fundamental meaning points to the subject's dependence on his own ego. The broadened meaning refers to the subject's intentional acts of volition, which are directed to values. While the former meaning of freedom stresses dependence, the latter points to independence. "For if we just want one thing or another—an X or a Y—then we experience an intentional directing toward the object as the freedom from compulsion or necessity: thus I may, but I need not, desire the object of my willing."[23] In this somehow dialectical reasoning, Wojtyła portrays human freedom as both dependence and independence. The former meaning, however, is more fundamental; it conditions and makes possible the latter.

Man experiences his own independence in relation to these objects [intentional objects of volition], since his actions are rooted in the fundamental de-

20. Cf. above, 102–3.
21. This section of *The Acting Person* develops Wojtyła's thoughts from *Love and Responsibility*, where he pointed out that self-determination draws the line between humans and animals (cf. *Miłość*, 25–26 [23–24]).
22. Cf. above, 117–18.
23. *Osoba*, 166 (120).

pendence on self. Realistic interpretation of freedom uses the model of auto-determinism instead of indeterminism. It is clearly visible in human experience that indeterminism assumes a secondary role while auto-determinism has primary and fundamental significance.[24]

Following the twentieth-century psychologists of the will, Wojtyła distinguishes two basic kinds of volitive acts, simple and expanded. In the former, the subject simply wants X; in the latter, he has to choose between X and Y. Wojtyła emphasizes, however, that in both kinds of volition, the essence of the human volitive act consists in a decision *(electio, rozstrzygnięcie)*. According to him, the presence of decision in every act of the human will points to the phenomenon of human freedom and, therefore, forms an experiential argument against anthropological determinism. "In true willing, the subject is never passively directed to an object. The object . . . never leads the subject back upon itself; it never forces the subject into its own reality thereby determining it from without; that kind of subject-object relation would in fact amount to determinism . . . The moment of decision in the human will rules out any such pattern of relation."[25]

In order to explore the topic of human choice and decision more deeply, Wojtyła focuses first on human motivation. He defines motivation as the effects that motives have on the will. In every act of "I want," the will strives toward an object that is presented to the person by the cognitive faculties as a good. This intentional movement of the will toward its end, a desired object, is indicated by the word "motive," which comes from the Latin term *movere,* "to move."

Wojtyła writes that it is the motive that defines the distinction

24. Ibid., 166 (my translation). The reader may have some difficulty in finding this important quotation in the English translation (cf. *The Acting Person,* 121), since the translator rewrote the whole paragraph currently under discussion.

25. Ibid., 172 (127).

between a simple act of will and an expanded one. In the former, there is only one value moving the will. In the latter, the will is presented with many attractive objects which are analyzed by the subject before anyone of them is chosen in a moment of decision *(rozstrzygnięcie)*.

> Choice always entails the renunciation of a spectrum of objects, of possible values, for the sake of one single object or value. It also necessitates putting off some potential willings for the actual one. This one willing together with the chosen value forms a whole, in which the dynamic essence of nature of the will—and indirectly also the person in his transcendence—is visualized in a special way.[26]

Giving an example of his fascinating phenomenological insight, Wojtyła indicates that during the process of deliberation of motives, there is a temporary suspension of the person's willing. This suspension reveals the vertical transcendence of the subject as well as his self-possession and self-governance. Wojtyła insists that the human will is not cramped by its objects. Rather, it is the will that determines and freely chooses an object as the end of its movement. This indeterminism of the human will, Wojtyła concludes, reveals the phenomenon of human freedom.

The analysis of the person's deliberation of motives points to another crucial topic, the relation between the will and cognition. In the moment of decision, Wojtyła writes, the will chooses one object among many alternatives because of the will's internal subordination to truth. The truth becomes the criterion of the will's choice. The truth also is an intrinsic principle of the will itself, as expressed in the traditional notion "*appetitus rationalis.*"[27]

---

26. Ibid., 176 (131).

27. John Paul II's criticism of the modern understanding of freedom points to a disappearance of the link between freedom and truth (cf. *Veritatis Splendor*, 32–34). He holds that this false theory of freedom is largely responsible for the terrible wars

According to Wojtyła, in the inner dynamism of the will, one discovers a twofold relation: an intentional relation to objects, and a relation to truth. Because of the will's subordination to truth, it is not determined by its objects but can choose between them. In the process of choosing one object among many, the will begins with a certain indetermination; i.e., it is ready to direct its intention to any one of the available goods. Because of its dependence on truth, the motivation moves the will from its initial, undetermined stage to a moment of free decision in which the will chooses one concrete object. This moment can be described as the will's and the person's self-determination. Only truth then, Wojtyła concludes, makes possible the subject's freedom of choice, his vertical and horizontal transcendence, and his self-determination.[28]

The person's cognition of the will's objects requires a further examination. Following the phenomenological tradition, especially Scheler's ethics, Wojtyła calls this cognition "an experience of value." He writes: "In the experience of value the moment of truth also seems to play an essential role. It is the truth about this or that object which crystallizes this or that moment of good. When for instance we experience the nutritive value of a food, we at once come to know

---

of the twentieth century, repeating the thesis of Leo XIII from his 1891 encyclical *Rerum Novarum* (cf. *Centessimus Annus*, 17). John Paul II warns that the modern alliance between human liberties and moral relativism may lead to alienation of the human person and, ultimately, to some new kind of totalitarianism (cf. *Centessimus Annus*, 44).

28. Wojtyła briefly remarks that the relation between the will and cognition is twofold. On the one hand, as was shown above, the will depends on cognition. On the other hand, cognition depends also on the will. Because of its natural dynamism, the will turns intentionally to the goods it encounters and then it "demands" from the intellect the truth about the encountered goods. The dependence of the practical cognition on the will, Wojtyła concludes, reveals a special character of this cognition (cf., *Osoba*, 185–86 [140–41]).

what is the good of the object, which serves us as food."[29] These three concise sentences, which Wojtyła does not elaborate any further, contain the conclusions of his precise and laborious analyses from the *Lublin Lectures*. In his second *Lublin Lecture,* "Good and Value," presented at the Catholic University in Lublin in the academic year 1955–56, Wojtyła confronts the theories of good created by Plato, Aristotle, St. Augustine, Thomas Aquinas, and Immanuel Kant with the phenomenological theory of values created by Max Scheler. His conclusions give another example of his attempt to create a phenomenological-metaphysical synthesis. On the one hand, following the existential metaphysics of Aquinas, Wojtyła accepts the ontological description of good as one of the three transcendentals. On the other, Wojtyła unmistakably likes Scheler's approach, where values are presented as the primary objects of the subject's willings. Therefore, Wojtyła creates a synthesis of good and value by defining value as "the good insofar as it offers itself to and for the integral being of the concrete person."[30] This definition of value from the *Lublin Lectures,* underlined by a phenomenological-metaphysical synthesis, allows Wojtyła to say in *The Acting Person* that in every experience of value, the subject learns the truth about the will's object, i.e., the good.

Wojtyła's theory of human volition deserves attention. The most interesting part of this theory, which makes it distinct from both Thomism and phenomenology, consists in a distinction between the two essential elements of the human will: intentionality and self-

29. Ibid., 186 (141).
30. Schmitz, *At the Center,* 56. Professor Schmitz points out two of Wojtyła's original contributions to metaphysical ethics. First, Wojtyła states that the distinctive character of the human ethical action consists in freedom. Secondly, Wojtyła uses the term "value," usually applied by some subjective theories, integrating it with his realistic metaphysics.

determination. The former element emphasizes the teleological structure of the will in relation to its objects; the latter points to the phenomenon of human freedom. Interestingly, Wojtyła describes freedom as both dependence and independence. On the one hand, the acts of human volition depend on the subject's ego; on the other, they have to be independent of values to which they are intentionally directed. Wojtyła emphasizes that acts of volition depend on the subject's cognition and, ultimately, on truth. Therefore, the subject's dependence on truth forms the *sine qua non* of human freedom.

Freedom of choice forms the core of Western liberal culture. By presenting in *The Acting Person* his own theory of freedom, Wojtyła began his profound dialogue with liberalism, which has continued throughout his whole pontificate. While emphasizing the essential link between freedom and truth, he points to the limitations of freedom. He also warns that if these limitations are crossed, human liberty can easily and destructively turn against itself.

Many contemporary thinkers have pointed out that postmodernism has brought a crisis in the idea of emancipation, which has dominated Western modern history.[31] In this time of crisis, John Paul II proposes a coherent and realistic theory of freedom, which not only avoids the mistakes of moral relativism and subjectivism but clearly rejects any kind of determinism and totalitarianism. By doing this, the Pope preserves and saves for the next generations the essence of Western civilization. Therefore, George Weigel is right when he calls John Paul II "the Pope of freedom."[32] It is possible that Karol Wojtyła will be remembered by this title.

---

31. Cf., Böckenförde, 235. Also: Jean-François Lyotard, *The Postmodern Condition: A Report on Knowledge* (Minneapolis: University of Minnesota Press, 1993), 31–41.

32. "The New 'New Things,'" in: *A New Worldly Order: John Paul II and Human Freedom*, ed. G. Weigel (Washington: Ethics and Public Policy Center, 1992), 20.

FULFILLMENT

Wojtyła insists that *The Acting Person* describes the human agent and his action not as two separate and self-sufficient realities but as a single, deeply cohesive reality. The person realizes and develops himself by acting, while the action most completely reveals the person. This cohesion of the person and the action, Wojtyła continues, is most adequately expressed in the notion of "the person's fulfillment in performing an action." The meaning of fulfillment *(spełnienie)* goes beyond the notion of the efficacy of the person, since it points out that in every action *(agere)* the agent fulfills himself. Therefore, the term "fulfillment" seems to be homologous with the Latin term "*actus*," which refers to a fullness corresponding to a certain potentiality *(potentia)* of the person.[33]

In every human action, the person is the cause, while the action appears as the consequence of the agent's efficacy. Wojtyła indicates that the person's efficacy can be seen in two different dimensions: (1) as internal or external, and (2) as transitive or intransitive. For example, a written letter is an external and transitive effect of a human action; a moral value of the person is an internal and intransitive effect. *The Acting Person* is concerned primarily with the latter. "Human actions once performed do not vanish without trace: they leave their moral value, which constitutes an objective reality intrinsically cohesive with the person, and thus a reality also profoundly subjective."[34] Morality, he continues, forms an existential whole with the human person. Also,

---

33. *Osoba*, 194 (149–50). *The Acting Person* is the first publication where Wojtyła presented his theory of human fulfillment. The other source where he outlined this theory is his article "Problem teorii moralności" (The problem of the theory of morality), published in 1969, when the first edition of *Osoba i czyn* also appeared (cf. "Problem teorii moralności," 238–43).

34. *Osoba*, 196 (151).

the axiological and normative dimension of morality is secondary to its ontological dimension, which points to the existential reality of the person who fulfills himself in an action. Therefore, Wojtyła writes that the true fulfillment of the person is accomplished not by a mere performance of every action but by the positive moral virtuality of the action. Respectively, an evil action brings a nonfulfillment of the acting person.

The axiological and ontological dimensions of morality reveal a contingency *(contingentia, przygodność)* of the human being. Every person has to make moral choices between a fulfillment achieved through good actions and a nonfulfillment brought by evil actions. In other words, the fundamental criterion of human fulfillment consists in truth, since the agent fulfills himself only through true goods.[35] Following the Christian tradition, Wojtyła calls the faculty in which the agent experiences the truth about goods, conscience. Also, he points out that the conscience is the place where the person experiences the moral duty to do something or to avoid doing something. "The function of conscience consists in distinguishing the element of moral good in the action and in releasing and forming a sense of duty with respect to this good. The sense of duty is an experiential form of the reference to (or dependence on) the moral truth, to which the freedom of the person is subordinate."[36]

Wojtyła goes on to present more extensively his theory of con-

35. In *The Acting Person,* Wojtyła repeatedly asserts his thesis that it is the subject's dependency on truth that provides the basis for his transcendence over reality, over all objects of cognition and volition. This relation of dependence on truth and the search for truth is characteristic primarily of the intellect and only secondarily of the mirroring and reflexive consciousness. Therefore, Wojtyła emphasizes that human transcendence is rooted in the intellect rather than in consciousness. He writes: "Far from being but a passive mirror that only reflects objects, man acquires through truth as a value a specific ascendancy over them" (ibid., 202 [159]).

36. Ibid., 199 (156).

science. He defines the conscience as "a judgement which indicates the moral value of an action."[37] The conscience can also be understood in a broader sense as "an entire effort of the person to grasp the truth in the domain . . . of moral values."[38] Wojtyła emphasizes that this effort of conscience to seek truth cannot be identified with a theoretical inquiry. Conscience refers to the praxis of the human person and, therefore, is intrinsically connected with the human will in its dynamics of self-determination.

Wojtyła's theory of conscience strikes us as very similar to that of Thomas Aquinas, who defined conscience as a judgment of practical reason.[39] In both theories, conscience consists in a practical cognition which is clearly distinguished from a theoretical inquiry of the human person. Also, both Wojtyła and Aquinas see the essential element of conscience in its relation to objective truth about human goods.

There are only two publications where Wojtyła presented his philosophical theory of conscience—his 1953 habilitation thesis and *The Acting Person*. In the former source, Wojtyła pointed out that Max Scheler failed to appreciate adequately the role of conscience in human action.[40] According to Wojtyła, this philosophical mistake can be attributed to Scheler's vehement and radical opposition to Immanuel Kant. Objectively, the active role of conscience can be known to the human agent through the experience of moral duty. Scheler totally excluded the notion of duty from his ethics and, therefore, he was not able to describe the human conscience.

In *The Acting Person*, Wojtyła avoids Scheler's mistake by outlining

37. Ibid., 203 (160).
38. Ibid. The latter definition points to the fact that an active search for and an inquiry into the truth is also part of the function of conscience.
39. Cf. Krąpiec, *I-Man*, 224–25.
40. Cf. Galarowicz, 68–71.

carefully the relation between conscience and the human experience of duty. He emphasizes that conscience is the place where the human agent experiences moral duty. Traditionally, the notion of duty, brought to prominence in ethics by Kant, has raised serious criticism among the representatives of Aristotelian-Thomistic thought.[41] The differences between the perfectionist and teleological ethics of the good and the ethics of duty are often seen by both sides as irreconcilable. Wojtyła does not share this skepticism of many of his colleagues; he believes in the possibility of a synthesis of these two positions. He wrote in his 1969 article: "It seems that the opposition between the ethics of value and the ethics of duty, which became dominant at the end of the nineteenth century, deforms the human experience of morality by placing an artificial emphasis on only one of its aspects. The goal of the theory of morality consists in a correct unification of these two aspects as found in human experience."[42]

There are other representatives of the phenomenological tradition who share Wojtyła's belief in a possibility of the synthesis between the theories of good and the theories of duty. One of them is Paul Ricoeur, who in a 1992 interview insisted that the modern encounter of these two theories presents the most important problem for contemporary ethics.[43] On the Thomistic side, Joseph Pieper holds that the notion of moral duty should be integrated into realistic moral philosophy. He insists that the basic principle of practical reason does not

41. On this subject there are many Polish articles and books, polemical in thrust. Cf., Stanisław Kamiński, "O strukturze etyki" (About the structure of ethics), in *Logos i Ethos: Rozprawy Filozoficzne* (Krakow, 1971), 267–78; Jerzy Gałkowski, "Spór o powinność moralną" (Dispute about moral duty), *Roczniki Filozoficzne* 20, no. 2 (1972), 5–39; Edward Kaczyński "Etyka powinności czy etyka decyzji" (Ethics of duty or ethics of decision), *Studia Theologiae Varsoviensis* 29, no. 2 (1991), 61–77.

42. "Problem teorii moralności," 240.

43. Paul Ricoeur, "Cóż to jest prawda?" (What Is Truth?), *Teofil* 1, no. 1 (1992), 84.

consist in the indicative or descriptive concept of good but rather in the command "you ought to love and do the good."[44]

In *The Acting Person,* Wojtyła emphasizes that ethical duty forms a fundamental experience of every human agent. This experience takes place in the conscience, where an opinion "X is truly good" is transformed into a practical command "I should perform the action that leads to a realization of X."[45] Through this transformation which results in an experience of duty, conscience becomes the source of moral norms. Wojtyła insists that his theory of moral norms does not lead to subjectivism, because conscience is constituted by its relation to objective truth. "The sense of the moral or legal normative sentences lies essentially in the truth of the good that they objectify. It is owing to their truthfulness that they become related to the conscience, which then, so to speak, transforms their value of truth into the concrete and real obligation."[46]

Wojtyła insists that because of its relation to truth, the moral duty in its normative function reflects the objective order of goods. Also, it is duty that serves as a bridge between human causal efficacy and human responsibility. Wojtyła writes that the agent is responsible for X only when he should have done X or should not have done X. The topic of responsibility, which goes beyond the scope of this book, is of particular importance for Wojtyła. He points out that the relation

---

44. Joseph Pieper, *Living the Truth: The Truth of All Things and Reality and the Good* (San Francisco: Ignatius Press, 1989), 154.

45. According to Wojtyła, the human ethical experience reveals a deep unity of "ought" and "is," two elements which were sharply contrasted by David Hume and his followers (cf. Alasdair MacIntyre, *A Short History of Ethics,* 169–177). Wojtyła holds that the conscience of every human agent experiences the intrinsic connection between the truth about the good ("is") and ethical duty ("ought") as necessary to the realization of the good.

46. *Osoba,* 207 (164).

between personal efficacy and responsibility can serve as a starting point for establishing the elementary facts on which rests the whole moral and legal order in its social dimension.[47]

Wojtyła's theory of human fulfillment forms an important part of his treatment of the acting person and human efficient causality. He pointed out that the person's fulfillment achieved through actions can be identified with the agent's happiness *(eudaimonia)*.[48] Therefore, his theory of human fulfillment can be seen as a new formulation and new approach to the Aristotelian-Thomistic eudaimonism.

In his 1967 programmatic article "Etyka a teologia moralna" (Ethics and moral theology), Wojtyła insisted that the fundamental task of contemporary ethics consists in justifying moral norms.[49] He insists on the same thing in *The Acting Person* by pointing out that the normative and axiological dimension of morality is rooted in its ontological dimension, i.e., the fulfillment of the acting person achieved through fully human, morally right actions *(agere)*.

For Wojtyła, human fulfillment is an objective category, since it can be achieved only through true human goods. That is why in his description of human ethical activity he assigns such an important role to conscience, which informs the agent about the objective truth of different goods and indicates the moral values of particular actions. In the normative conscience, the agent also experiences the moral duty to do something or to avoid doing something. Wojtyła's synthesis of the notion of duty with his teleological and perfectionist ethics of good is possibly the most interesting aspect of his theory of human fulfillment.

47. Ibid., 211–16 (169–74).
48. Ibid., 216–17 (174–75).
49. *Aby Chrystus,* 464–65.

INTEGRATION

Wojtyła's theory of transcendence led him into a dialogue with the nineteenth- and twentieth-century German philosophy of human freedom. He was aware, however, that a large part of this philosophy treats the human person from a dualistic and idealistic perspective. What is required, therefore, for a complete and successful explication of his theory of the acting person is an account of the human body and an explanation of the role that human biology and physiology play in *actus humanus.* Wojtyła provides this explanation in his theory of integration.

Wojtyła first introduced the notion of integration into his philosophy in *Love and Responsibility.* In the section "Psychological Analysis of Love," he describes how personal acts of love integrate different layers and dimensions of the subject and how different human dynamisms reveal their full meaning in acts of love.[50] In *The Acting Person,* Wojtyła develops and explains more fully the notion of integration. He points out that transcendence reveals only one aspect of human self-possession and self-governance. "The concept of 'self-possession' denotes the person both as the one who possesses himself and as the one who is in possession of himself. Similarly, the concept of 'self-governance' denotes the person both as the one who governs himself and as the one who is in a way subjected and subordinate to himself."[51]

Human transcendence denotes this aspect of self-possession and self-governance which consists of one's possession of himself and of one's governance. Integration *(integratio, integracja)* denotes a reality of the person that is complementary to transcendence. This reality is described by expressions such as "being in possession" and "being sub-

50. *Miłość,* 92–106 (101–19).
51. *Osoba,* 230 (190).

jected and subordinate to himself." Wojtyła indicates that, etymologically, the word "integration" is derived from the Latin adjective "*integer*," which means whole, complete, unimpaired. Correspondingly, the philosophical term "integration" is defined as "the realization and the manifestation of a whole and a unity emerging on the basis of some complexity."[52] The psychosomatic complexity of the human person is integrated into a unity and a whole in every human action (*agere, czyn*). Wojtyła emphasizes, however, that human action is more than just a sum of other dynamisms. It is rather a new and superior dynamism, in which all the others receive a new meaning and a new quality that is properly personal. Therefore, only because of the person's integration in the action is one provided with an adequate insight into and comprehension of the human psychosomatic complexity.

Wojtyła begins a more precise analysis of integration with the description of the person's soma. The somatic element refers to the human body, which can be described in two dimensions, in regard to its outerness and to its innerness.

The body is material, it is a visible reality, which is accessible to sense; the access to it is first of all from the "outside." The outer shape of the human body determines, in the first place, what is visible in man; it decisively affects his individual appearance and the definite impression that he makes. So conceived, the human body is composed of different members, each of which has its place and performs its proper function.[53]

52. Ibid., 231 (191). Wojtyła also gives a more detailed definition of integration: "The integration of the person in the action indicates a very concrete and, each time, a unique and unrepeatable introduction of somatic reactivity and psychical emotivity into the unity of the action—into the unity with the transcendence of the person expressed by efficacious self-determination that is simultaneously a conscious response to values" (267 [225]). This definition uses two notions crucial to Wojtyła's philosophy, somatic reactivity and psychical emotivity, which will be defined in the following pages.

53. Ibid., 241 (200–201).

Besides the outerness, Wojtyła writes, the human body has also its own innerness, which denotes the diversity and mutual coordination of the bodily organs. He points out that, because of the body, the human person is part of nature. Therefore, there are many similarities between man and other parts of nature, especially animals, as well as many connections and influences. Because of these direct connections between the human body and nature, Wojtyła describes the character of the person's somative dynamisms as reactive, i.e., able to react to external stimuli. All the other strata of the person, e.g., psyche or emotions, are only indirectly connected with nature, by means of the somatic dynamisms.

Wojtyła emphasizes that the somatic dynamism does not depend on the person's self- determination, because its source does not consist in the human will but rather in the instinctive and spontaneous reactions of the body. Therefore, the somatic dynamism cannot be described as "man-acts" *(agere)* but as "something-happens-in-man" *(pati).*[54] Since they happen on the level of nature, somatic activations are not present in the person's experience of his own efficient causality.[55] Also, the dynamism of the human soma often operates outside of consciousness. He concludes:

We can see that within the frame of the integral subjectivity of the person . . . the body seems to have a somewhat separate "subjectivity" of its own—without, however, affecting in any way the ontic unity of man. Its subjectivity thus exists only in the sense that the body as such is the subject solely of reactions; hence its subjectivity is reactive, vegetative, and external to consciousness.[56]

Central to Wojtyła's theory of integration is the thesis that the goal of the process of integration consists in a matching of the reactive

---

54. Cf. above, 102–3.   55. Cf. above, 105–6.
56. *Osoba,* 252 (212).

subjectivity of the body with the efficacious and transcendental subjectivity of the person. Through this process of integration, the somatic activations are incorporated into the person's self-possession, self-governance, and self-determination.

In Wojtyła's anthropology, the term "psyche" *(psychika)* refers to all manifestations of human life that are in themselves not bodily or material. They do reveal, however, some dependence on the body, some somatic conditioning. Eyesight or emotions are examples of the person's psychic activities. Wojtyła emphasizes that because of their complex interdependence and cooperation, the soma and the psyche should not be understood as totally separate entities. It is important, however, to make a clear distinction between them. The psyche, for instance, is not material in the sense that the body is. All psychical functions of the person are internal and immaterial. While they depend on the soma, they cannot be reduced to it.

Wojtyła defined the somatic dynamism as reactive. Correspondingly, he defines the psyche as emotive. Etymologically, the words "emotive" and "emotivity" point to a movement or a motion which originates inside the subject, as is indicated by the prefix *"ex."*[57] Somatic reactivity consists in the ability of the body to react to external stimuli. Emotivity also seems to react to external impulses, e.g., a beautiful mountain view or a great painting by a nineteenth-century French impressionist. In the case of emotivity, however, the internal effects of those external impulses transcend purely bodily reactions and result in feelings *(czucia).*[58] Thus, according to Wojtyła, the main difference between the reactive soma and the emotive psyche is that

57. Ibid., 265–66 (224).

58. For Wojtyła, feelings *(czucia)* and emotions *(uczucia)* are two different notions which denote two distinct psychic phenomena. To feelings he attributes a certain cognitive function not present in emotions.

the somatic impulses do not exceed the potentiality of the body, while in the case of feelings, this potentiality is transcended both in quality and in essence. He continues: "Through feelings, man emerges from and above . . . the 'subjectivity of the body.' While such 'subjectivity' is in itself closely related to the somatic reactivity and to a large extent remains unrecorded in consciousness, the psychical subjectivity, which emerges together with feelings on the basis of the body, is already included in consciousness."[59]

According to Wojtyła, through feelings alone the somatic reactivity becomes present in the mirroring and reflexive consciousness. Therefore, through feelings man can experience his own body. For example, often through pain one experiences one's internal organs—stomach or liver—which functions ordinarily are not mirrored in consciousness. Feelings become a bridge between unconscious somatic reactions and consciousness.[60]

Wojtyła emphasizes that the person's experience of his own body, which is a result of many different feelings, does not reveal the separate "subjectivity" of the body, but rather points to the somatic structure of the whole subject, of the whole ego. This personal holistic experience of one's own body he defines as self-feeling *(samo-poczucie)*. He writes: "The direct and proper object of self-feeling is the whole somatic ego, which is not isolated from the personal ego but is, on the contrary, intrinsically cohesive with it."[61]

59. *Osoba*, 269 (228).

60. Wojtyła indicates the existence of a certain precedence of consciousness over feelings. The subject is usually conscious of the feelings, except in a case of an "emotionalization of consciousness," but the opposite is not true. One does not have a "feeling of consciousness." According to Wojtyła, this precedence of consciousness over feelings is the *sine qua non* condition of personal self-determination as well as self-possession and self-governance.

61. Ibid., 271 (229). The experience of one's body is not the only instance in which feelings are mirrored by consciousness. Man not only feels his body but also has a more

To human feelings he attributes a certain cognitive function which consists of the subject's sensitivity *(wrażliwość)*. Etymologically, both in English and in Polish, sensitivity is related to sensation *(wrażenie)*, which in turn points to sense-perception. Wojtyła insists, however, that human sensitivity does not possess a purely sensory character, but is deeply rooted in the intellectual and spiritual life of the person. At the same time, sensitivity has a primarily receptive character and, therefore, should be integrated into the person's self-determination.

Wojtyła explains the cognitive function of feelings by pointing out that they are directed intentionally to values. For example, the person's self-feeling manifests a distinctive, qualitative trait and value element, as is evident in expressions like "I feel well today" or "I do not feel well." Wojtyła insists that this emotive experience of values should be subordinated to the objective truth about values as cognized by the person's intellect.

Integration of the person in the action refers essentially to truth which makes possible an authentic freedom of self-determination. Therefore, experience of values, which is a function of man's sensitivity itself (and hence also a function of feelings), must, within the dimension of the acting person, be subordinated to the reference to truth. The fusion of sensitivity with truthfulness is the necessary condition of the experience of values. It is only on the basis of such an experience that authentic choices and decisions can be formed.[62]

For Wojtyła, human sensitivity is not the ultimate criterion of values or the sole basis for the personal experience of values. The integration of feelings and emotionally experienced values into the subject's self-determination has to occur in relation to truth, since

---

general feeling of himself as well as feelings about other people and many other objects in the surrounding world. Wojtyła emphasizes that the mirroring of these different feelings by consciousness determines the subject's experience of his own ego as being-in-the-world.

62. Ibid., 275 (233).

only then is the subject's transcendence safeguarded. Correspondingly, a person's sole reliance on feelings excludes the possibility of self-determination, which requires an active cooperation of the person's will and intellect.

Two other terms which play an important role in Wojtyła's anthropology are excitement *(podniecenie)* and stirring emotion *(wzruszenie)*. Excitement is an emotive activation *(emotywne uczynnienie)* rooted in the somatic reaction of the body, e.g., faster breathing and quickened heartbeat. The difference between excitement and other human feelings consists in the excitement's lack of any cognitive function. Excitement rather seems to reveal at its core a connection with the human appetites *(appetitus)* and volitive desires.

Wojtyła's term "*wzruszenie*" denotes a psychic phenomenon different from excitement. The latter seems to be much more linked to the person's somatic reactivity, whereas the former is "a manifestation of a pure emotivity" and "an activation of the psyche itself in which somatic underlayers are less clearly pronounced."[63] Therefore, in "*wzruszenie*," bodily feelings give priority to spiritual feelings, which may have aesthetic, ethical, or religious character.

Wojtyła goes on to define the term "emotion": "We have been speaking about different emotions, of different manifestations of man's affectivity. At their root there is always a stirring of emotion *(wzruszenie)*; this emotive core may be said to be radiating internally and thus to produce every time a different emotional experience. It is this experience that we call "emotion."[64] He indicates that emotions are not an effect of the subject's conscious efficacy but rather happen spontaneously *(pati)* in the person. By describing the spontaneous character of emotions, he emphasizes their independence from the

63. Ibid., 281 (239).
64. Ibid., 281 (239–40).

proper efficacy of the person, i.e., the subject's self-determination. This independence places before the subject a special task of integrating the spontaneous efficacy of his emotions into the personal structure of self-possession, self-governance, and self-determination. This integration is possible is because the force of emotions derives from the experience of value.

Wojtyła insists that the emotions' reference to values is neither cognitive nor appetitive. He writes that "emotions . . . point to values but as such they have no cognition nor desire of values."[65] Rather, it is due to feelings *(czucia)* that the subject gains some cognition of values, which are only passively indicated by emotions. According to Wojtyła, however, the ultimate cognition of emotionally experienced values should come through the exercise of the human intellect *(rozum)*, which he defines as "[man's] power and ability to be guided in choice and decision by the truth itself about the good."[66] It is the intellect that reconciles the person's spontaneous emotivity with his conscious transcendental efficacy in the process of integration.

Human proficiencies *(habitus, sprawność)* play an important role in the process of integration. He notes: "It lies in the nature of proficiencies to aim at subordinating the spontaneous emotivity of the subjective ego to its self-determination. Their way to achieve this end, however, is to make the best use of emotive energy and not to suppress it."[67]

According to Wojtyła, the human will, supported by proficiencies, aims to restrain the spontaneous explosion of emotive energy and even to assimilate some of it. If successfully completed, this process results in two effects important for the person's process of integration.

65. Ibid., 289 (248).
66. Ibid., 291 (249). Wojtyła's insistence on the role of intellect in the cognition of values can be seen as part of his polemics with Max Scheler. According to the German phenomenologist, material values are cognized primarily through the subject's emotions.
67. *Osoba*, 294 (253).

First, when properly assimilated, the emotive energy considerably strengthens the energy of the will itself. Second, through proficiencies, the will adopts the spontaneity and ease of functioning which are characteristic of emotion. Therefore, in regard to values, the will is able to choose the good and to reject the bad spontaneously, as indicated by the subject's feelings and "approved" by the intellect.

* * *

Wojtyła's account of integration forms one of the most original parts of his theory of the acting person. In order to describe adequately human integration, he applies his own philosophical categories such as *pati* and *agere*, the phenomenological and metaphysical understanding of human nature and subjectivity, the subject's self-determination, mirroring and reflexive consciousness. Using his poetic and phenomenological ability to describe the nuances of human phenomena, with the theory of integration, Wojtyła introduces in his anthropology two new notions, somatic reactivity and psychic emotivity, which form the basis of his theory of human soma and psyche.

Wojtyła, an actor, poet, and playwright, was particularly well prepared to create an adequate theory of human affectivity. He does not base his theory, however, purely on poetic sensitivity but draws extensively on other sources: philosophy, psychology, medicine, biology. Among the philosophical sources, two of them are clearly distinguishable: Aquinas's theory of *passiones animae* and Scheler's theory of emotional cognition of values. Regarding Aquinas, Wojtyła shares him the conviction that emotions should be subjected to the will guided by the intellect and that this subjection is the function primarily of proficiencies and virtues.[68] Scheler, on the other hand, helped

---

68. in *The Acting Person*, Wojtyła does not make a clear distinction between proficiencies and virtues.

Wojtyła, to appreciate the richness of human emotions and their role in the process of value cognition.[69] Balancing the Thomistic emphasis on human rationality and Scheler's emphasis on human affectivity, Wojtyła, in *The Acting Person,* presents a convincing understanding of soma and psyche.

The theory of integration forms an important part of Wojtyła's account of human efficient causality. In accord with universal human experience, he is able to describe the somatic and psychic activations *(pati)* which participate in the dynamization of human nature, often outside of consciousness and the subject's conscious activity. While rejecting anthropological dualism and idealism, Wojtyła presents a convincing description of the human intellect and the will which, strengthened by virtues, integrate the somatic and psychic "happenings" into the subject's self-determination and his conscious efficient causality.

According to Wojtyła, integration is a complementary aspect of human transcendence. Transcendence points to the subject's primacy and superiority over the objects of his cognition and volition, due to the phenomenon of human freedom and self-determination. In the theory of integration, however, Wojtyła reminds the reader that the human person remains a part of nature due to his soma and psyche. Therefore, for every human person, transcendence remains always a challenge and a goal to be achieved only through the painstaking, creative, and personal effort of integration.

69. In his third *Lublin Lecture,* "The Problem of Norm and Happiness," Wojtyła writes that Scheler's theory of emotions is an important contribution to the history of philosophy. After Scheler, the simplistic and shallow understanding of human happiness and pleasure that is typical for hedonism and utilitarianism is no longer possible (cf. *Wykłady,* 282, 288–89).

CHAPTER 6

Conclusions

THE SUBJECT OF this book, the human person as the efficient cause of his own action, locates the very center of Wojtyła's philosophy. One reason for this is the intrinsic unity and constant interrelation of anthropology and ethics in the thought of Wojtyła. In his anthropological publications, he always analyzes the ethical implications of the anthropological theses. Correspondingly, when he writes about ethics, he is always interested in the question: "What concept of man underlies a particular ethical theory?" I have been able, therefore, to explore the fundamental themes of Wojtyła's anthropology and ethics while at the same time safeguarding the unity of these two philosophical disciplines—a unity so characteristic of Wojtyła.

This unity of anthropology and ethics is present in Wojtyła's earliest publications, including his poetry. For example, his 1944 poem "Song of the Hidden God" describes the internal transformation of a Christian believer who has encountered God. The 1950 poem, "Song of the Brightness of Water," continues the same theme, reflecting upon the New Testament encounter of the Samaritan woman with Jesus Christ at the well of Sychar. Both poems are also the starting point for Wojtyła's theological anthropology, which found its mature formulation in John Paul II's *Wednesday Catecheses on the Theology of the Body* and his encyclicals. In both poems, anthropological and ethical descriptions penetrate, enlighten, and supplement each other.

Wojtyła's first philosophical publications systematize his poetic intuitions. In the 1951 article "About the Humanism of St. John of the Cross," he attempted to extract a philosophical picture of man from the theology of the *Doctor Mysticus*. The other article from the same year, "Mystery and Man," elaborates the anthropological conclusions of the theological doctrine of Christ's Incarnation. In Wojtyła's philosophy, anthropology and ethics maintain a fruitful exchange.

As we saw, the problem of human efficient causality emerged explicitly for the first time in Wojtyła's 1953 habilitation dissertation. One of our aims has been to assess the compatibility of the ethical system of the German phenomenologist Max Scheler and revealed Christian ethics, for Wojtyła's first encounter with the phenomenological tradition was possibly the single most formative event in his intellectual career.

In the context of the post-World War II period, Wojtyła's work on Scheler was very important, because Scheler was regarded by many Catholic thinkers as an influential ally in the confrontation with Kantian philosophy, which denied the human intellect any access to ontic reality. There were some striking similarities between the Christian worldview and Scheler's philosophy: an emphasis on love, appreciation of religion, the importance of following an ethical example, and a reverence for human virtues. However, in regard to the question whether the philosophical ethics of Scheler can be used to interpret revealed Christian morality, Wojtyła gives a negative answer. He argues that the differences between Scheler and Christian thought are much more significant and fundamental than are any superficial similarities. Wojtyła's reasoning provides a good, critical insight into Scheler's ethics while at the same time laying a foundation for his own theory of human efficient causality.

Let us briefly summarize his position. First, Wojtyła argues that in Scheler's ethics, ethical values do not have a practical character, i.e., there is no link between ethical values and the subject's actions. Wojtyła insightfully points out that this link can be sufficiently illuminated only when the person is described as the efficient cause of his own actions. Scheler, however, deliberately avoids the problem of human efficient causality, because of two methodological reservations. First, he holds that values are never known intellectually by the subject but rather are experienced emotionally. Second, because of his phenomenological method, Scheler is able to analyze the agent only as a unity of feelings but not as a complex being or as a substance in the process of change.

In his habilitation thesis, Wojtyła contends that the theory of human efficient causality also requires an adequate account of human conscience. It is conscience, a subjective norm of morality, which obliges the subject to act according to objective norms. According to Wojtyła, however, Scheler did not recognize the important role of conscience in human actions because of his anti-Kantian endeavor to exclude any kind of obligation from ethics. For Scheler, an ethical obligation is always associated with a negative value. In attempting to eliminate any kind of negativism from ethics, he rejects the notion of ethical duty. It is true, Wojtyła writes, that obligation often has a negative character in the subject's emotional life. However, in the informed acts of the will, obligation is present in a positive and creative way. Wojtyła concludes that, because he excludes obligation from ethics, not only is Scheler unable to explain the essence of the religious and moral commandments present in Christian Revelation, he is also unable to describe human efficient causality, since it always includes an experience of obligation.

Hence, Wojtyła formulates an important principle of his philosophy of the acting person. In order to describe adequately the phenomenon of human love, one has to describe the link between ethical obligation and the subject's willing of values. Immanuel Kant's and Max Scheler's descriptions of this connection were both one-sided. Kant reduced love to an experience of duty and reverence for law; Scheler excluded ethical duty from ethics in favor of the subject's experience of values. According to Wojtyła, however, both ethical duty and experience of value form important elements of human ethical life. Since the early 1950s, this conviction has become one of the cornerstones of his philosophy of the acting person and of his account of human efficient causality.

In the conclusions of his habilitation thesis, Wojtyła emphasizes the usefulness of the phenomenological method for ethics. He is aware, however, that its usefulness is limited. It can describe the person's experience of ethical values but it cannot define the objective principle which decides why a human act is morally right or wrong. In order to define this principle, one has to place ethical values in the objective order of the good. Wojtyła emphasizes that this is possible only through a metaphysical analysis. Therefore, a Catholic ethicist can use the phenomenological method, but he cannot be a phenomenologist.

Earlier, we recounted how Wojtyła's important insights and opinions gathered during his studies on Scheler were submitted to the test of the history of philosophy during his 1954–57 *Lublin Lectures*. Wojtyła held that moral obligation is a part of universal human experience and, therefore, has to be appreciated and explained by a moral philosopher. The research of twentieth-century experimental psychology strengthened his conviction that human efficient causality is also a part of the agent's experience and, therefore, must be described and analyzed according to the phenomenological method. The most significant part of the *Lublin Lectures*, however, consisted in his renewed appreciation of the thought of Thomas Aquinas. Wojtyła first encountered that thought during his 1946–48 studies at the Angelicum in Rome. Most of his subsequent philosophical and theological publications reveal the strong influence of the Doctor Angelicus. Nonetheless, it was during the *Lublin Lectures* that Wojtyła appropriated and integrated some theses of Aquinas into his own anthropology and ethics.

Aquinas's most significant contribution to Wojtyła's theory of human efficient causality consists in the concept of the rational will. According to Thomas, the will has the ability to move spontaneously toward everything that is good *(bonum in communi)*. In this striving toward good, however, the will is directed by the intellect, which, by presenting different desirable goods, "helps" the will to choose a concrete good as an actual goal of its desire. Wojtyła emphasizes that this becoming of the will must be described in terms of ethical values. Everything else in the human person is morally right or morally wrong insofar as it depends on the will, since the will is the efficient cause of the subject's becoming and the actualization of the will always implies an actualization of the whole subject.

The *Lublin Lectures'* exercises in the history of philosophy also helped Wojtyła to define his own philosophical method. This method was used for the first time in his analysis of human love in *Love and Responsibility* and then, ten years later, systematically presented in the introduction to *The Acting Person*. Wojtyła's method consists of two steps: phenomenological description, and metaphysical synthesis. Phenomenology is useful as a starting point for anthropology and ethics, Wojtyła holds, because of its ability to discover and describe many aspects of the human phenomenon which otherwise would be unknown to a metaphysician. As we saw, however, in *The Acting Person*'s analyses of *agere* and *pati*, efficacy and subjectivity, person and nature, any phenomenological description is in need of a synthesis, since it considers the human person under many aspects. Such a synthesis can be obtained only through a metaphysical analysis which is able to describe the ultimate roots of all the phenomenological aspects of the human phenomenon.

Wojtyła's philosophical method aims to describe and interpret human experience fully. In *The Acting Person*, therefore, he presents his own theory of experience. He holds that human experience consists of two steps, induction and reduction. The former involves a transition from the multiplicity and complexity of existential data to a grasping of their essential sameness. Reduction involves retrieving what is irreducibly given in an experience by outlining the most fundamental principles of an experienced object. Hence, in his epistemology, Wojtyła takes a realist position. He believes that the knowing subject is able to distinguish naturally between what exists and what does not. According to Wojtyła, the transcendence of experienced objects over the intellect of the knowing subject is a necessary condition for the existence of objective truth.

His methodology is one of the most debated and criticized areas of his philosophy. Because he attempted to create a synthesis between phenomenology and metaphysics, Wojtyła became vulnerable to criticism and misunderstanding from both sides. Thus, phenomenologists often hold that does not pursue the phenomenological investigation far enough; neo-Thomists criticize him for his use of phenomenological method, as well as for his limited application of metaphysics.

Some legitimate questions about the method do, however, arise, and they point to the need for further studies. For example, the relation between Wojtyła's understanding of induction and Aristotle's needs to be explained. Can the method of induction be applied in the same way, as Wojtyła seems to suggest, to a description of external phenomena as to a description of the subject's inner experience and consciousness? If not, what are the differences? One may also question whether Wojtyła's method of reduction can be understood simply as retrieving the causes *(arche, causa)* which for centuries formed the method of classical philosophy. While it is difficult to deny Wojtyła's thesis about experiential origins of metaphysical notions, this position requires further analyses, which he does not provide. These and other questions leave Wojtyła's methodology open for further investigation and specification.

Wojtyła presents his mature theory of human efficient causality in his *opus magnum, The Acting Person,* and in some articles published after 1969. Since the phenomenon of human causality reveals itself most completely in the conscious acts of the person, he introduces first his theory of consciousness. This theory manifests the methodological and epistemological assumptions that mark his philosophical differences with classic phenomenology, modern idealism, and twentieth-century neo-Thomism.

According to Wojtyła, the fundamental function of consciousness consists in a mirroring of the objects that are already known to the subject through his knowledge and self-knowledge. The other important function of consciousness, called by Wojtyła the "reflexive" function, brings into prominence in human experience the subjectiveness of the subject. Through the reflexive function of consciousness, the human subject experiences his own actions and moral values in relation to his own ego. Correspondingly, he experiences himself as the efficient cause of actions.

Reflection on the relation between consciousness and different kinds of human activity led Wojtyła to distinguish two fundamental kinds of human activity: (1) man acts *(agere)*, and (2) something that is happening in man *(pati)*. In the former, the subject is the conscious cause of his own actions; in the latter, there is a passive dynamization of the subject's nature. Thus, Wojtyła emphasizes the limits of consciousness by describing human dynamisms that are not mirrored by consciousness, e.g. the somato-vegetative processes and the subconsciousness. He indicates that every anthropology which is limited exclusively to an analysis of consciousness does not describe the whole person.

Wojtyła's theory of human transcendence and self-determination forms the core of his treatment of the person's efficient causality. He defines human self-determination as the relation between the agent and his will, wherein the person is constituted by the activity of his will. Self-determination reveals the person's vertical transcendence, since the agent, depending on his will, is never determined totally by the external objects of his cognition and volition. Therefore, personal self-determination points to the phenomenon of human freedom. Wojtyła's theory of vertical transcendence and self-determination is designed to supplement and deepen the Aristotelian-Thomistic analysis of human volition. Wojtyła holds that this analysis is one-sided, because it remains too focused on intentional willing directed toward an external object.

He emphasizes that human self-determination points to a certain objectification of the subject, since in every actual act of self-determination—in every "I will"—the self becomes the primary object of will. He writes that, in contrast with the intentional acts of the will, the acts of self-determination do not possess an intentional character. By rejecting the intentionality of self-determination, he attempts to emphasize a certain lack of distance between the objectivity and subjectivity of the human agent as opposed to the distance created by the human will directed intentionally to its other objects.

Thus, Wojtyła presents an interesting theory of human freedom which later laid the foundation for John Paul II's teaching in such documents as *Centessimus Annus, Veritatis Splendor,* and his *"Letter to Families."* In *The Acting Person,* Wojtyła distinguishes two meanings of human freedom. The fundamental meaning points to the subject's self-determination and, therefore, his dependence on his own ego. The broadened meaning refers to the subject's intentional acts of volition which are directed toward values. Having defined freedom as both dependence and independence, Wojtyła emphasizes that the former definition is more fundamental, conditioning and making possible the latter.

According to Wojtyła, the phenomenon of freedom can be experienced by every person in an expanded act of will. In such an act, the subject has to make a decision *(rozstrzygnięcie)* in order to chose between two different objects of volition. The universal human experience indicates that the subject is not determined by these objects. Rather, in the process of self-determination, the will freely chooses one object among many alternatives. In this process, the will is guided by the intellect, which presents the will with the truth about different values (goods). The truth then becomes the criterion of the will's choice. Wojtyła insists that only truth makes possible the subject's freedom of choice, his vertical and horizontal transcendence, and his self-determination.

Following the Christian tradition, Wojtyła calls the faculty in which the agent experiences the truth about goods, conscience. Also, he points out that the conscience is the place where the person experiences moral duty to do or to avoid doing something. Thus, in the conscience, an opinion "X is truly good" is transformed into a practical command "I should perform the action that leads to a realization of X." In his theory, the conscience becomes the place where different philosophical theories—the perfectionist and teleological ethics of the good, the phenomenological ethics of value, and the ethics of duty—have to converge in order to describe adequately the role of conscience in the *actus humanus.*

Wojtyła was aware that a large part of nineteenth- and twentieth-century German philosophy treats the human person from a dualistic and idealistic perspective. Therefore, what was required for a complete and successful explication of his theory of the acting person was an account of the human body and an explanation of the role that human biology and physiology play in human activity. In his theory of integration in *The Acting Person* he provides this explanation.

Wojtyła defines integration as an introduction of somatic reactivity and psychic emotivity into the unity of the *actus humanus,* i.e., the unity of the transcendence and efficacious self-determination of the subject. In regard to the human soma, Wojtyła indicates that within the frame of the integral subjectivity of the person, the human body possesses a somewhat separate "subjectivity" of its own which is reactive, vegetative, and often external to consciousness. Thus, the goal of the process of integration consists in a matching of the reactive subjectivity of the body with the efficacious and transcendental subjectivity of the person. In regard to the human psyche, human sensitivity and emotions have to be integrated into the subject's self-determination through a subjection to truth. Wojtyła insists that only truth makes possible the freedom and vertical transcendence of the agent.

His theory of human efficient causality is far from completion. Even his *opus magnum, The Acting Person,* in some sections looks more like a first draft or an outline of a book than a comprehensive study. It seems that his time-consuming pastoral and administrative responsibilities as the Bishop of Cracow took a heavy toll in the area of his academic career. Still, his philosophy of the acting person deserves attention and applause.

Wojtyła strikes us as a master of synthesis and as one who is able to learn from others. In critical encounters with the great thinkers of Western civilization—Plato, Aristotle, Augustine, Aquinas, Immanuel Kant, Max Scheler—he is able to take from their theories some elements in order to incorporate them into his own system. Also, to describe adequately the human phenomenon, he creatively uses his own philosophical categories like *pati* and *agere,* the phenomenological and metaphysical understanding of human nature and subjectivity, the subject's self-determination, and the mirroring and reflexive functions of consciousness. From this emerges a compelling picture of the acting person.

Many have already asked the question, whether history will honor John Paul II with the title "the Great." George Weigel points out that twice in the history of Christianity popes have been so named:

Like John Paul II, Leo and Gregory led a Church confronted by the claims of barbarians: in Leo's case, the Huns; in Gregory's, the Lombards. Leo the Great successfully turned Attila back from Rome; Gregory the Great effected a truce with the invading Lombards and set about the work of converting them to orthodox Christianity.[1]

If history comes to think of Wojtyła as "John Paul the Great," Weigel argues, the reasons will have much to do with a third successful papal intervention in the face of the barbarians. This time, the barbarians are the modern and post-modern "masters of suspicion," whose radical deconstruction of reason poses a grave threat to Western civilization. To oppose such barbarians, John Paul II created his Christian anthropology, his theory of the acting person.

1. *Soul of the World: Notes on the Future of Public Catholicism* (Grand Rapids, Mich.: Eerdmans, 1996), 96–97.

BIBLIOGRAPHY

PRIMARY SOURCES

"Boże Narodzenie 1958" (Christmas 1958). In *Aby Chrystus*, 67–75.

Człowiek w polu odpowiedzialności (Man in the field of responsibility). Lublin: Instytut Jana Pawła II, 1991.

"Elementarz etyczny" (Elements of ethics). In *Aby Chrystus*, 127–182.

"Etyka a teologia moralna" (Ethics and moral theology). In *Aby Chrystus*, 462–69. Thomism is the best model for applying a philosophical theory as a means of interpreting the Catholic Church's moral teaching. However, some modifications should be made in Thomistic anthropology and ethics, e.g. (1) in ethics, the normative dimension should be emphasized more than the teleological; (2) Thomistic anthropology should be supplemented with a theory of consciousness; and (3) there is a need for a new interpretation of the Thomistic theory of virtues.

"Instynkt, miłość, małżeństwo" (Instinct, love, marriage). In *Aby Chrystus*, 36–50. The sexual drives play an important role in building a marital relationship. However, in order to serve a lasting commitment, sexual drives have to be purified by the virtue of chastity.

Miłość i odpowiedzialność (Lublin: Wydawnictwo Towarzystwa Naukowego Katolickiego Uniwersytetu Lubelskiego, 1986). English translation: *Love and Responsibility*, trans. H. T. Willetts. New York: Farrar, Straus, Giroux, 1981.

"Myśli o małżeństwie" (Thoughts about marriage). In *Aby Chrystus*, 414–24.

"Natura i doskonałość" (Nature and perfection). In *Aby Chrystus*, 140–42.

"Natura ludzka jako podstawa formacji etycznej" (Human nature as fundamental for ethical formation). *Znak* 11, no. 6 (1959), 693–97.

"O humanizmie św. Jana od Krzyża" (About the humanism of St. John of the Cross). In *Aby Chrystus*, 387–402.

Ocena możliwości zbudowania etyki chrześcijańskiej przy założeniach systemu Maksa Schelera (On the possibility of constructing a Christian ethics on the

basis of the system of Max Scheler). Lublin: Towarzystwo Naukowe Katolickiego Uniwersytetu Lubelskiego, 1959.

Osoba i Czyn. In *Osoba i czyn oraz inne studia antropologiczne* (The acting per-
son and other anthropological studies), pp. 43–345. Lublin: Wydawnictwo
Towarzystwa Naukowego Katolickiego Uniwersytetu Lubelskiego, 1994).
English translation: *The Acting Person,* trans. A. Potocki, rev. Anna-Teresa
Tymieniecka. Boston: Reidel, 1979.

"Osoba, podmiot i wspólnota" (Person: subject and community). *Roczniki Filozoficzne* 24, no. 2 (1976), 5–39.

"Personalizm Tomistyczny" (Thomistic personalism), in: *Aby Chrystus,* 430–
42. In a brief summary of the main themes of Thomistic anthropology,
Wojtyła emphasizes that historically, philosophical personalism originated
in the theological reflections of the Church Fathers and early Councils. He
criticizes Descartes as the father of modern anthropological dualism.

"Problem doświadczenia w etyce" (The problem of experience in ethics).
Roczniki Filozoficzne 17, no. 2 (1969), 5–24.

"Problem oderwania przeżycia od aktu w etyce na tle poglądów Kanta i Schelera" (The problem of separating an experience from an act in the ethical
theories of Kant and Scheler). *Roczniki Filozoficzne* 5, no. 3 (1957), 113–40.
This article presents a summary of Wojtyła's criticism of the ethical theories of Immanuel Kant and Max Scheler, which was extensively presented in
his first *Lublin Lecture,* "Ethical Act and Ethical Experience." Wojtyła postulates the need for a synthesis of a formal ethics of duty and a phenomenological ethics of value.

"Problem teorii moralności" (The problem of the theory of morality). In *W
nurcie zagadnień posoborowych* (In the current of post-conciliar issues).
(Warszawa, 1969), 217–49.

"Problem uświadomienia z punktu widzenia teologii" (The problem of sexual
awareness from a theological point of view). *Ateneum Kapłańskie* 64, no. 1
(1962), 1–5.

"Problematyka dojrzewania człowieka" (The problem of human maturation). *Nasza Rodzina* 9, no. 2 (1977), 2–15.

"Realizm w etyce" (Realism in ethics). In *Aby Chrystus,* 137–40.

"Religijne przeżywanie czystości" (Religious experience of chastity). In *Aby
Chrystus,* 51–61.

"Rodzina jako *communio personarum*" (The family as *communio personarum*). *Ateneum Kapłańskie* 66, no. 3 (1974), 347–61.

"Rozważania pastoralne o rodzinie" (Pastoral reflections about the family).
Roczniki Nauk Społecznych 3 (1975), 59–76.

Sign of Contradiction. New York: The Seabury Press, 1979.

"Słowo końcowe" (Concluding remarks). *Analecta Cracoviensia* 5–6 (1973–74), 243–63.

Sources of Renewal: The Implementation of the Second Vatican Council. San Francisco: Harper & Row, 1979.

"The Structure of Self-Determination as the Core of the Theory of the Person." In *Tommaso D'Aquino nel suo Settimo Centenario: Atti del Congresso Internazionale (Roma-Napoli—17/24 Aprile 1974).* Napoli: Edizioni Domenicane Italiane, 1978.

"Subjectivity and the Irreducible in Man." *Analecta Husserliana* 7 (1978), 107–14.

"System etyczny Maksa Schelera jako środek do opracowania etyki chrześcijańskiej" (The ethical system of Max Scheler as a means to an interpretation of Christian ethics). *Polonia Sacra* 6, no. 4 (1955), 143–61.

"Tajemnica i człowiek" (Mystery and man). In *Aby Chrystus,* 28–35. All of the different strata of being present in the universe converge in the person, who manifests physical as well as organic, psychic, and spiritual dimensions. The mystery of Jesus Christ's Incarnation leads man to discover his true place in the universe and the meaning of his life.

"Właściwa interpretacja nauki o szczęściu" (The proper interpretation of the teaching about happiness). In *Aby Chrystus,* 156–58.

Wykłady lubelskie (Lublin lectures). Lublin: Wydawnictwo Towarzystwa Naukowego Katolickiego Uniwersytetu Lubelskiego, 1986.

"Wychowanie miłości" (Education of love). In *Aby Chrystus,* 88–92. Truly human love can be reached only at the end of a long educational process in which the intense but short-lived sexual emotions are integrated with the person's intellect and will.

"Zagadnienie katolickiej etyki seksualnej" (The topic of Catholic sexual ethics). *Roczniki Filozoficzne* 13, no. 2 (1965), 5–25.

Zagadnienie wiary w dziełach św. Jana od Krzyża. Kraków: Wydawnictwo o.o. Karmelitów Bosych, 1990. English translation: *Faith According to Saint John of the Cross,* trans. Jordan Aumann. San Francisco: Ignatius Press, 1981.

"Zagadnienie woli w analizie aktu etycznego" (The problem of will in the analysis of the ethical act). *Roczniki Filozoficzne,* no. 1 (1957), 111–35. This is a brief presentation of some contemporary problems regarding the philosophy of human will. Wojtyła treats these problems extensively in his first Lublin Lecture, "Ethical Act and Ethical Experience."

"Znaczenie powinności" (The meaning of duty). In *Aby Chrystus,* 142–46.

ANTHOLOGIES OF WOJTYŁA'S WRITINGS

Aby Chrystus się nami posługiwał (To serve Christ). Kraków: Znak, 1979.
Collected Poems, trans. Jerzy Peterkiewicz. New York: Random House, 1979.
The Collected Plays and Writings on Theater, trans. Bolesław Taborski. Berkeley: University of California Press, 1987.
Poezje i dramaty (Poetry and drama). Kraków: Znak, 1979.

JOHN PAUL II'S DOCUMENTS
QUOTED IN THIS BOOK

The Apostolic Letter *Tertio Millenio Adveniente*. Washington: United States Catholic Conference, 1994.
Crossing the Threshold of Hope. New York: Alfred A. Knopf, Inc., 1994.
The Encyclical *Centessimus Annus*. Washington: United States Catholic Conference, 1991.
The Encyclical *Evangelium Vitae*. Washington: United States Catholic Conference, 1995.
The Encyclical *Laborem Exercens*. Washington: United States Catholic Conference, 1981.
The Encyclical *Veritatis Splendor*. Washington: United States Catholic Conference, 1993.
"Letter to Families" for the International Year of the Family. Washington: United States Catholic Conference, 1994.
"List do Wielkiego Kanclerza KUL abpa Bolesława Pylaka" (Letter to the Grand Chancellor of KUL Abp. Bolesław Pylak). In *Księga Pamiątkowa w 75-o lecie KUL*, pp. 9–10. Lublin: Redakcja Wydawnictw Katolickiego Uniwersytetu Lubelskiego, 1994.
Mężczyzną i niewiastą stworzył ich. Odkupienie ciała a sakramentalność małżeństwa. Città del Vaticano: Libreria Editrice Vaticana, 1986. The English translation of this book appeared in three separate volumes: *Original Unity of Man and Woman: Catechesis on the Book of Genesis; Blessed Are the Pure of Heart: Catechesis on the Sermon on the Mount and the Writings of St. Paul;* and *Reflections on Humanae Vitae: Conjugal Morality and Spirituality*. All volumes published by Daughters of St. Paul: Boston, 1980, 1983, and 1984.
To the Youth of the World: Apostolic Letter of Pope John Paul II on the Occasion of International Youth Year. Washington, D.C.: United States Catholic Conference, 1985.

SECONDARY LITERATURE ON WOJTYŁA

Blazynski, George. *John Paul II: A Man from Krakow.* London: Weidenfeld and Nicolson, 1979.

Buttiglione, Rocco. "Kilka uwag o sposobie czytania *Osoby i czynu*" (Some remarks about how to read *The Acting Person*). In Wojtyła, *Osoba i czyn oraz inne studia antropologiczne*, 11–42.

Elson, John. "Man of the Year." *Time* 144, no. 26 (1944), 63–73.

Frossard, Andre. *"Be Not Afraid!": Pope John Paul II Speaks Out on His Life, His Beliefs, and His Inspiring Vision for Humanity.* New York: St. Martin's Press, 1984.

Galarowicz, Jan. *Człowiek jest osobą Podstawy antropologii filozoficznej Karola Wojtyły.* (Man is person. The foundations of philosophical anthropology of Karol Wojtyła). Kraków: Wydawnictwo Naukowe Papieskiej Akademii Teologicznej, 1994.

Gogacz, Mieczysław. "Hermeneutyka osoby i czynu. Recenzja książki Kardynała Karola Wojtyły *Osoba i czyn.*" (Hermeneutics of person and action. A review of the book *The Acting Person* of Cardinal Karol Wojtyła). *Analecta Cracoviensia* 5–6 (1973–74), 125–39.

Gramatowski, Władysław, and Zofia Wilińska. *Karol Wojtyła w Świetle publikacj: Bibliografia* (Karol Wojtyła in the light of publications: Bibliography). Citta del Vaticano: Libreria Editrice Vaticana, 1980.

Gray, Paul. "Empire of the Spirit." *Time* 144, no. 26 (1994), 53–57.

Grygiel, Stanisław. "Hermeneutyka czynu oraz nowy model swiadomości" (Hermeneutics of action and a new model of consciousness). *Analecta Cracoviensia*, 5–6 (1973–74), 139–51.

Jaworski, Mieczysław. "Koncepcja antropologii filozoficznej w ujęciu kardynała Karola Wojtyły. Próba odczytania w oparciu o studium *Osoba i czyn*" (Cardinal Karol Wojtyła's concept of philosophical anthropology: an attempt at interpretation of *The Acting Person*), *Analecta Cracoviensia*, 5–6 (1973–74), 91–106.

Johnson, Paul. *Pope John Paul II and the Catholic Restoration.* New York: St. Martin Press, 1981.

Kalendarium życia Karola Wojtyły (Diary of life of Karol Wojtyła), ed. Adam Boniecki. Kraków: Znak, 1983.

Kalinowski, Jerzy. "Metafizyka i fenomenologia osoby ludzkiej. Pytania wywołane przez *Osobę i czyn*" (Metaphysics and phenomenology of the human person: questions raised by *The Acting Person*). *Analecta Cracoviensia*, 5–6 (1973–74), 63–71.

Kamiłski, Stanisław. "Jak filozofować o człowieku?" (How to think philosophically about man). *Analecta Cracoviensia*, 5–6 (1973–74), 73–79.

Keller, Józef. "Zwodnicze rozwiązanie źle postawionego problemu," (Deceptive solution to a falsely formulated problem). *Studia Filozoficzne* 1 (1961), 201–3.

Krąpiec, Mieczysław. "Książka kardynała Karola Wojtyły monografią osoby jako podmiotu moralności" (The book of Cardinal Karol Wojtyła as a monograph of person as a subject of morality). *Analecta Cracoviensia*, 5–6 (1973–74), 57–61.

Maliński, Mieczysław. *Pope John Paul II: The Life of Karol Wojtyła*. New York: The Seabury Press, 1979.

Obecność. Karol Wojtyła w Katolickim Uniwersytecie Lubelskim (Presence. Karol Wojtyła at the Catholic University in Lublin). Lublin: Redakcja Wydawnictw KUL, 1989.

Półtawska, Wanda. "Koncepcja samoposiadania—podstawą psychoterapii obiektywizującej. W świetle książki Kardynała Karola Wojtyły *Osoba i czyn*" (The concept of self-possession as the basis for an objective psychotherapy: in the light of *The Acting Person* by Cardinal Karol Wojtyła). *Analecta Cracoviensia*, 5–6 (1973–74), 223–41.

Saward, John. *Christ Is the Answer: The Christ-Centered Teaching of Pope John Paul II*. New York: Alba House, 1995.

Schmitz, Kenneth L. *At the Center of the Human Drama: The Philosophical Anthropology of Karol Wojtyła/Pope John Paul II*. Washington: The Catholic University of America Press, 1993.

Stróżewski, Władysław. "Książki o etyce" (Books about ethics). *Znak* 2 (1961), 272–75.

Styczeń, Tadeusz. "Metoda antropologii filozoficznej w *Osobie i czynie* kardynała Karola Wojtyły" (The method of philosophical anthropology in *The Acting Person* by Cardinal Karol Wojtyła). *Analecta Cracoviensia*, 5–6 (1973–74), 107–15.

Swieżawski, Stefan. "Karol Wojtyła na Katolickim Uniwersytecie Lubelskim" (Karol Wojtyła at the Catholic University in Lublin). In *Obecność. Karol Wojtyła w Katolickim Uniwersytecie Lubelskim* (Lublin: Redakcja Wydawnictw KUL, 1989).

Szczypka, Józef. *Jan Paweł II. Rodowód* (John Paul II: Origins). Warszawa: Instytut Wydawniczy Pax, 1990.

Szulc, Tad. *Pope John Paul II: The Biography*. New York: Scribner, 1995.

Urmanowicz, Walenty. *Ateneum Kapłańskie* 3 (1961), 279–84.

Weigel, George. "The New 'New Things,'" in: *A New Worldly Order: John Paul*

II and Human Freedom, ed. G. Weigel. Washington: Ethics and Public Policy Center, 1992.

————. *Soul of the World: Notes on the Future of Public Catholicism.* Grand Rapids, Mich.: Eerdmans, 1996.

Williams, H. George. *The Mind of John Paul II: Origins of His Thought and Action.* New York: Seabury Press, 1981.

Woznicki, N. Andrew. *A Christian Humanism: Karol Wojtyła's Existential Personalism.* New Britain: Mariel Publications, 1980.

GENERAL LITERATURE

Aristotle. *The Complete Works of Aristotle.* 2 volumes. Ed. Jonathan Barnes. Princeton: Princeton University Press, 1984.

Augustine. *Confessions.* Trans. Henry Chadwick. Oxford: Oxford University Press, 1991.

Böckenförde, Ernst-Wolfgang. *Wolność—państwo—Kościół* (Liberty—state—church). Kraków: Znak, 1994.

Bourke, Vernon. *Will in Western Thought: An Historico-Critical Survey.* New York: Sheed and Ward, 1964.

Decrees of the Ecumenical Councils. Ed. Norman P. Tanner. Washington: Georgetown University Press, 1990.

de Lubac, Henri. *At the Service of the Church.* San Francisco: Ignatius Press, 1993.

————. *Surnaturel: études historiques.* Paris: Aubier, 1946.

Dihle, Albrecht. *The Theory of Will in Classical Antiquity.* Berkeley and Los Angeles: University of California Press, 1982.

Frings, Manfred. *Max Scheler: A Concise Introduction into the World of a Great Thinker.* Pittsburgh: Duquesne University Press, 1965.

Gałkowski, Jerzy. "Spór o powinność moralną" (Dispute about moral duty). *Roczniki Filozoficzne* 20, no. 2 (1972), 5–39.

Garrigou-Lagrange, Reginald. *Christian Perfection and Contemplation According to St. Thomas Aquinas and St. John of the Cross.* London: Herder Book Co., 1937.

————. "Saint Thomas et Saint Jean de la Croix," *La Vie Spirituelle,* n. 10 (1930), 16–37.

Kaczyński, Edward. "Etyka powinności czy etyka decyzji" (Ethics of duty or ethics of decision). *Studia Theologiae Varsoviensis* 29, no. 2 (1991), 61–77.

Kahn, Charles. "Discovering the Will: From Aristotle to Augustine." In I. M. Dillon and A. A. Long, *The Question of "Eclecticism": Studies in Later Greek Philosophy.* Berkeley: University of California Press, 1988.

Kamiński, Stanisław. "O strukturze etyki" (About the structure of ethics). In *Logos i Ethos. Rozprawy Filozoficzne*, pp. 267–78. Kraków, 1971.

Kant, Immanuel. *Critique of Practical Reason*. Trans. H. W. Cassirer. Milwaukee: Marquette University Press, 1998.

———. *Grounding for the Metaphysics of Morals*. Trans. James W. Ellington. Indianapolis: Hackett Publishing Company, 1993.

Kenny, A. J. P. *Aristotle's Theory of the Will*. New Haven: Yale University Press, 1979.

Krąpiec, Mieczysław. *I-Man: An Outline of Philosophical Anthropology*. New Britain: Mariel Publications, 1983.

Lescoe, J. Francis. *Philosophy Serving Contemporary Needs of the Church: The Experience of Poland*. New Britain: Mariel Publications, 1979.

Lyotard, Jean-François. *The Postmodern Condition: A Report on Knowledge*. Minneapolis: University of Minnesota Press, 1993.

MacIntyre, Alasdair. *After Virtue: A Study in Moral Theory*. Notre Dame: University of Notre Dame Press, 1981.

———. *A Short History of Ethics*. New York: Macmillan, 1966.

———. *Three Rival Versions of Moral Enquiry: Encyclopaedia, Genealogy, and Tradition*. Notre Dame: University of Notre Dame Press, 1990.

Maritain, Jacques. "The Cultural Impact of Empiricism." In *From an Abundant Spring*, pp. 448- 67. New York: Kenedy & Sons, 1952.

———. *The Degrees of Knowledge*. New York: Scribner's, 1959.

McCann, Leonard A. *The Doctrine of the Void as Propounded by St. John of the Cross in His Major Prose Works and as Viewed in the Light of Thomistic Principles*. Toronto: The Basilian Press, 1955.

McCool, A. Gerald. *The Neo-Thomists*. Milwaukee: Marquette University Press, 1994.

Nowa Encyklopedia Powszechna PWN. Ed. Barbara Petrozolin-Skowrońska. Warszawa: PWN, 1995.

Pieper, Joseph. *Living the Truth: The Truth of All Things and Reality and the Good*. San Francisco: Ignatius Press, 1989.

Pinto de Oliveira, Carlos-Josaphat. *Contemplation et Liberation: Thomas d'Aquin—Jean de la Croix—Bartolome de Las Casas*. Paris: Editions du Cerf, 1993.

Ricoeur, Paul. "Cóż to jest prawda?" (What Is truth?), *Teofil*, 1 (1992), n. 1, 84.

Scheler, Max. *Formalism in Ethics and Non-Formal Ethics of Values: A New Attempt toward the Foundation of an Ethical Personalism*. Trans. Manfred S. Frings and Roger L. Funk. Evanston: Northwestern University Press, 1973.

————. *Gesamelte Werke.* Ed. Maria Scheler (Bern: Francke Verlag, 1954–69) and Manfred S. Frings (Bonn: Bouvier Verlag, 1985–).

Schmidt, Hans. *Organische Aszese.* Paderborn, 1938.

Schmitz, Kenneth L. *What Has Clio to Do with Athena? Etienne Gilson: Historian and Philosopher.* Toronto: Pontifical Institute of Mediaeval Studies, 1987.

Shook, Laurence K. *Etienne Gilson.* Toronto: Pontificial Institute of Mediaeval Studies, 1984.

Smith, Janet. *Humanae Vitae: A Generation Later.* Washington D.C.: The Catholic University of America Press, 1991.

Spiegelberg, Herbert. *The Phenomenological Movement: A Historical Introduction.* 2 vols. The Hague: Martinus Nijhoff, 1960.

Suttor, Timothy. "Essence and Existence." Appendix in Thomas Aquinas, *Summa Theologiae.* London: Blackfriars, 1964–81.

Thomas Aquinas. *Summa Theologiae.* London: Blackfriars, 1964–81.

Tillmann, Fritz. *Die Katolische Sittenlehre: Die Idee der Nachfolge Christi.* Düsseldorf, 1939.

Voelke, A. J. *L'idée de volonté dans le stoïcisme.* Paris: Presses Universitaires de France, 1973.

INDEX

Destined for Liberty: The Human Person in the Philosophy of Karol Wojtyla/John Paul II
was composed in Minion by Generic Compositors, Stamford, New York; printed on
60-pound Writers Natural and bound by Thomson-Shore, Dexter, Michigan; and
designed and produced by Kachergis Book Design, Pittsboro,
North Carolina.

Printed in the United States
36440LVS00002B/343-441